SINGIN' IN THE RAIN

······················

Peter Wollen

BFI PUBLISHING

First published in 1992 by the
BRITISH FILM INSTITUTE
21 Stephen Street, London, W1P 2NL

Copyright © Peter Wollen 1992

Reprinted 2001

British Library Cataloguing in Publication Data

Wollen, Peter
　　Singin' in the Rain. (BFI Film Classics Series)
　　I. Title　II. Series
　　791.43

ISBN 0–85170–351–8

Designed by
Andrew Barron and Collis Clements Associates

Typesetting by
Fakenham Photosetting Limited, Norfolk

Printed in Great Britain by
Norwich Colour Print

CONTENTS

· ·

In Memory of Paddy Whannel

1

··

The history of cinema coincides with that of twentieth-century dance. In the first decade of our century, dance was revolutionised. Diaghilev and his choreographer, Fokine, changed the course of ballet, making it into a contemporary form which could survive the collapse of the *ancien régime*. Isadora Duncan set the agenda for the amazing expansion of 'modern dance'. And, it should not be forgotten, Bert Williams and George Walker launched the cakewalk, took black vernacular dancing out of the circumscribed world of the minstrel show, and laid the foundations of modern tap and show dancing.

When historians look back on this astounding revolution in one of the most ancient of the arts, they will be dependent for their research on choreographic notation, which was developed during the same period, on verbal description by critics and dancers, and, most important of all, on photography, film and video – pre-eminently, on film. On one level, film has served as a recording medium for dance performance and as such has played a crucial role in preserving twentieth-century dance, although even then, tragically, an enormous amount has simply been lost. Very little of the work of the Ballets Russes is on film, for instance. But, on another level, as film itself developed as an art form, it intersected with dance to create a new phenomenon – film dance, dance created expressly for film, with camera, framing and editing in mind.

The single most memorable dance number on film is Gene Kelly's solo dance 'Singin' in the Rain', in the film of the same name, which he co-directed in 1951, with Stanley Donen, for the Freed Unit at MGM. Despite a bumpy opening, when the film was shunted aside after its premiere in April 1952 in order to make way for the re-release of MGM's *An American in Paris*, which swept the Oscars later the same month, it nonetheless turned out to be an enormous popular and box-office hit. In time, it also enjoyed an acknowledged critical success, eventually reaching the number four slot in *Sight and Sound*'s 1982 fiftieth anniversary poll of world critics' 'Ten Best Lists', placed behind only Orson Welles's *Citizen Kane*, Jean Renoir's *La Règle du jeu*, and Akira Kurosawa's *The Seven Samurai*.

'Singin' in the Rain' is an aesthetically complex production. Kelly was the performer, the choreographer and, with Donen, the director. Carol Haney assisted with the choreography. The music for the song was written by Nacio Herb Brown and arranged for the film by Roger Edens. The lyrics were by Arthur Freed (also the producer), adapted by Kelly, who added 'and dancin'' to the title line. The cinematographer was Harold Rosson, who had worked with Kelly and Donen before, filming *On the Town* for them in 1949. They had specifically requested that Rosson replace John Alton, who had originally been assigned to the picture, following his success with *An American in Paris*, which starred Kelly but was directed by Vincente Minnelli, whose style was very different. Finally, of course, many other people were involved in countless other ways.

It is worth looking a bit more closely at what actually happened on and off the set to produce the sequence. First, Kelly knew that somewhere in the film, as the star, he should have a featured solo dance. The script, by Betty Comden and Adolph Green, had been written over a year before, while Kelly was busy working on *An American in Paris*;

Gene Kelly, Rita Hayworth and Phil Silvers in *Cover Girl*

and, although it was written with him in mind, it did not specify any particular number for his solo. In fact, 'Singin' in the Rain' is placed in the same position in their script, after the disastrous preview of *The Duelling Cavalier*, but they envisaged it as a number for the trio of Don Lockwood (Kelly), Cosmo Brown and Kathy Selden, who at that time were still uncast. The scene would begin, not outside Kathy's house as in the finished film, but in a restaurant, and the trio would dance off their stools out into the street and the rain, in an atmosphere of 'impromptu fun'. This idea was basically a reprise of the 'Make Way for Tomorrow' number which Kelly, Rita Hayworth and Phil Silvers had danced in *Cover Girl* (1944). Here too the three of them dance out of a restaurant and along the street, up and down the stoops, ducking into doorways to avoid a disapproving policeman, having fun with props on the way.

Although Kelly decided to make 'Singin' in the Rain' his solo, the trio was retained as the credit sequence for the film, a number now partly based on its very first film appearance in *Hollywood Review of*

The credit sequence of *Singin' in the Rain*

1929. But Kelly does still retain some key elements of 'Make Way for Tomorrow': not only the dancing down the street, but also details such as the suspicious cop. The main concept of the dance, however, now comes from the lyrics of the song. As he himself put it, 'It's got to be raining and I'm going to be singing. I'm going to have a glorious feeling, and I'm going to be happy again'.[1] This illustrative approach to dance is not as obvious as it sounds. It depended on the song being placed at a point in the story where glorious feelings were appropriate, and thus on the integration of the dance number into the narrative.

On one level, *Singin' in the Rain* can be seen as a backstage musical, whose story basically boils down to 'putting on a show', as in the cycle of Judy Garland–Mickey Rooney musicals Busby Berkeley made for the Freed Unit in its earlier years. Now, instead of amateur theatricals in the barn, the show is the first musical picture being made at Monumental, a fictional Hollywood studio. However, unlike the conventional 'putting on a show' musical, in *Singin' in the Rain* the musical numbers are not limited to the film within the film but also occur at regular intervals within the framing story, built round the relationships between the major characters. They are stitched into the dramatic action. The 'Singin' in the Rain' sequence is not just an entertainment interlude, it is conceived as an expression of Don Lockwood's feelings at a particular point in both his professional and his personal life.

This preoccupation with the 'dramatic integrity' of the dance numbers derives, to an important extent, from developments in the Broadway stage musical. In the early 1940s the operetta and the musical comedy developed a new vision, whereby dances were integrated into the drama as expressions of characters' moods and feelings, rather than slotted in simply as opportunities for spectacular dancing. This development coincided with the shift of responsibility for dances from a 'dance director', responsible for spectacle, to a 'choreographer', responsible for dramatic dance. In the end, the choreographer, instead of being a subordinate, began to be the major figure in the production of a musical, and Kelly's own example, in the cinema, contributed significantly to this trend. On Broadway, the decisive step is usually attributed to Agnes De Mille, for her work as choreographer of *Oklahoma!* in 1943.

In fact, this change within the Broadway musical reflected a change in American ballet: the inauguration of a specifically American style of choreography, dealing with American subjects and dramatising the dancing. In the spring of 1938, Lincoln Kirstein's American Ballet Caravan had put on an All-American Evening in New York, featuring *Show Piece* with music by Robert McBride and choreography by Martha Graham's star dancer, Erick Hawkins; *Yankee Clipper*, with music by Paul Bowles and choreography by Eugene Loring; and *Filling Station*, with music by Virgil Thomson and choreography by Lew Christensen. In all three of these ballets the choreographers were also the dancers. They were soon followed up by two ballets with music by Aaron Copland, Loring's *Billy the Kid*, in October 1938, and De Mille's *Rodeo* in October 1942, which led directly to *Oklahoma!*, followed by Leonard Bernstein and Jerome Robbins's *Fancy Free* in April 1944, which was then transformed into the stage musical *On the Town* by Comden and Green later the same year.

This period in American dance history was also the period in which Gene Kelly left his native Pittsburgh, arriving to work in New York in August 1938, before moving on to Hollywood in November 1941 and directing his first film, *On the Town*, too many years later, in 1950. As soon as he arrived at the Freed Unit, Kelly began agitating to get new choreographers out to Hollywood from New York, as well as experimenting with the new choreography in his own numbers. Particularly, he was interested in Eugene Loring, who was brought out to the Freed Unit in 1943 and went on to work on Minnelli's *Yolanda and the Thief*, and, much later, as choreographer of *Funny Face* and *Silk Stockings*.

Kelly, however, came originally out of tap rather than ballet. In Pittsburgh his father had been a phonograph record salesman who, ironically enough in the light of *Singin' in the Rain*, was put out of work by the slow-down of the record industry which followed the Crash, the rise of radio and the arrival of sound film. The Kelly family took up a new career, running a popular dance school in the Pennsylvania steel town of Johnstown. Kelly's early experiences of performance were of tap dancing with his brother Fred and his sister Louise, who eventually dropped out, leaving Gene and Fred as a brothers act. It is interesting that, unlike Astaire, Kelly never danced with a regular female partner, and generally seemed to prefer male partners. Astaire, of course, began dancing with his sister Adele, whereas Kelly worked his way up with his brother Fred. They began in working men's clubs, Moose Clubs, American Legion halls and so on, before graduating to vaudeville and 'presentations' (dancing with on-stage bands) and finally putting on their own shows. But, while still based in Pittsburgh, Kelly took a series of summer ballet classes in Chicago, studying with Kotchetovsky, who had been the partner and husband of Nijinska. In dance terms he was, so to speak, determined to be upwardly mobile, adding a ballet carriage and arm movements above the waist to tapping feet below.

Kelly's experience in New York strengthened the inclination to dramatise his dance. His first important role was as Harry the Hoofer in Saroyan's play *The Time of Your Life*, which opened in October 1939. This was Saroyan's follow-up to *The Great American Goof*, the 'ballet-play' choreographed by Eugene Loring, who also danced the lead. Harry was one of a motley crew of bums, sailors, prostitutes and drifters frequenting a waterfront bar. Kelly commented later:

> I realised that there was no character – whether a sailor or a truck driver or a gangster – that couldn't be interpreted through dancing, if one found the correct choreographic language. What you can't have is a truck driver coming on stage and doing an *entrechat*. Because that would be incongruous – like a lady opening her mouth and singing bass. But there was a way of getting that truck driver to dance that would not be incongruous – just as there was a way of making Harry the Hoofer, a saloon bum, look convincing. It may seem obvious now, but at the time it was an important discovery for me.[2]

Saroyan saw Kelly as like a Chorus in the play, the rattle of whose taps 'was not unlike a drum roll at a funeral', while at the same time Harry was trying to cheer up the other barflies with his hoofing.

His success as Harry the Hoofer, the part of a dancer in a straight play, got Kelly the role which first made him a star, as Joey in the Rodgers and Hart musical *Pal Joey*, which opened the following autumn. Here too he was playing a hoofer, this time a heel living off his appeal to women and exploiting them and anyone else for whatever he can get. It was unusual for a musical in its pessimism and dark view of its central character, but again it gave Kelly an opportunity to develop a dramatic role through his dancing. John Martin, the critic of the *New York Times*, wrote that 'the whole production is so unified that the dance routines are virtually inseparable from the dramatic action'. Robert Alton, the dance director for the production, was Kelly's principal sponsor in the city. He had spotted Kelly in Pittsburgh and it was because of his invitation that Kelly had come to New York. In due course Alton too came out to the Freed Unit, where he became the most employed dance director, working with Kelly again on *The Pirate* and *Take Me Out to the Ball Game*. Alton's ambitions pointed the way towards the integration of choreographer with stage or film director. In 1934 he had already developed a desire to 'pick up pointers in straight direction with the goal of ultimately directing the book and the dances of a musical comedy.'[3] He was the major influence on Kelly's career, in the sense that he both discovered Kelly and crystallised the nature of his ambition.

Tap dancing had always had a dimension of 'character dancing', but this was mainly for purposes of comedy. Kelly moved character dancing into the dramatic mainstream. At the same time, in tension with the drive towards integration, he stayed loyal to his roots in tap. Tap dancing differs from most other forms of dancing in that it appeals to the ear as well as the eye. In fact it is defined by the rhythmic sound of the metal taps on heel and toe, which distinguish it from its neighbours, clog and softshoe dancing. During the 1930s, tap dancers, such as the Nicholas Brothers or Fred Astaire, would have radio spots. Indeed, Astaire describes how he had to adjust his style for radio, where he was unable to cover ground or go up in the air and had to concentrate instead on 'a lot of taps close together – a string of ricky-ticky-ticky-tacky-ticky-tacky-taps'. He developed a repertoire of exhibition taps that included, for instance, 'a half-falling half-standing-up flash that sounded like a riveting machine'.[4] The Nicholas Brothers did a more musical rhythm-based act in the Cab Calloway radio show. There is an amazing range in the sound quality of tap performers – complex rhythm and syncopation, percussion, 'tonation', glides and slides, depending on floor surface, tap materials and so on.

Gene Kelly's 'Singin' in the Rain' sequence can be looked at (or listened to) as a novelty tap number in terms of its sound. Its predecessor in this respect is the 'Squeaking Board' dance which Kelly did as his solo in *Summer Stock* the year before. The dance director was Nick Castle, the Hollywood tap choreographer for dancers as dissimilar as Shirley Temple and the Nicholas Brothers. Kelly got extra time to plan this solo because Judy Garland was not showing up for a while and he went to discuss it with Castle, who demonstrated the sound made by tapping on a piece of newspaper. Kelly took up the idea, adding the sound of tearing, and experimenting with different qualities of newsprint before he eventually settled on old copies of the *Los Angeles Times* more than three months out of date as giving the best effect. However, he still needed another kind of sound as counterpoint and, after trying crunching pebbles and kicking cans, he finally settled on a squeaky board: 'I asked myself: where is the dance set? In a wooden barn. What's it like dancing in a barn? Difficult. Why? Because of the uneven floorboards. And that was when it hit me. A squeaky floorboard!'[5]

In 'Singin' in the Rain' the sound effects are caused by the rain and the pools of water. There is a background noise of the hiss of rain falling, accompanied by the squelchy sound of the taps. This eventually escalates to the gushing sound of the water-spout and the louder, sploshing noise made by Kelly jumping up and down in the puddles. Holes were specially dug on the sidewalk and filled up with water (six puddles), precisely where Kelly's choreography demanded them, and a lake was dug out in the gutter of the street. In fact, the whole number, which was shot out of doors on one of the permanent streets built on the studio back lot (East Side Street), demanded complex engineering to deliver the right flow of water through a series of pipes for the rain and the downspout. The area was also blacked out with tarpaulins (rather than shooting 'day for night') and had to be lit from behind so that the rain was visible in the glare from the carbon arcs and to avoid reflections in the shop windows. (In the opening and closing downpour sequences of *Rashomon*, Kurosawa added ink to the rain to make it more visible and I have been told that a similar method was used in *Singin' in the Rain*.)

Kelly further dramatised the dance in the rain by giving his movements a childish exuberance and glee, combined with his usual athleticism. He explained that to help him create the right mood, he 'thought of the fun children have splashing about in rain puddles and decided to become a kid again during the number.' In fact, a lot of Kelly's dancing has a feeling of childish fun and fooling to it. It must be relevant too that he spent so many years teaching children to dance at the family school in Johnstown and Pittsburgh. It is as if he identified with the children in the ambivalence between the discipline and hard work required to get dance steps perfect and the anarchic pleasure, underlined by the disapproving look of the policeman, which comes from stomping in puddles and hippety-hopping along the kerb. Kelly is also proud of the dance sequence he did for Gregory La Cava's *Living in a Big Way* in 1947, where he choreographed a complicated sequence with more than a dozen children – 'Ring Around the Rosie', the first part of which was based on children's games, such as hopscotch, seesaw, bouncing balls and rolling hoops, moving on to an acrobatic solo which used the frame and railings and rafters and pulleys and ladders of a half-built house, the children gazing up from beneath. This was the Kelly film for which Martha Graham praised his choreography, a compliment he later returned in praising her early work for its impact on him as a young man.

The effect of the 'Singin' in the Rain' sequence would be incomplete without Kelly's attention to the filming of the dance and its staging for the camera. Kelly began thinking about film dance right from his first appearance on film, in Busby Berkeley's *For Me and My Gal*, made in 1942. Kelly had a difficult relationship with Berkeley. Berkeley, like many Hollywood dance directors, including Alton, did not dance or choreograph himself. He dreamed up and staged dance numbers and left the choreography to others. Berkeley, of course, was an extremely innovative director. He was proud of planning each shot for a single camera, with long takes and continuity between shots, at a time when musicals were filmed with multiple cameras and incessant cutaways to different angles. He was incredibly inventive in thinking up new 'homogeneous quadrangle equations', as he called his geometrical schemas, on which to base his spectacular sequences. As he put it, 'It was hard to think up an original number because I never brought someone out from the side of the wings and then they went into their dance. Never in my life. That's the old way.'[6] In 1953, for the 'Gotta

Hear that Beat' number in *Small Town Girl*, he conceived the idea of burying eighty-six musicians under the stage, with hundreds of holes for their arms cut through the floor for them to play their instruments. They wore white and the floor and backdrop were painted grey. Berkeley had to decide where to put the holes. 'I had to lay out in my mind each shot, in my office, so that the camera would make certain angles and turns.' Ann Miller actually had to dance the sequence, tapping through the forest of arms and the rows of saxophones and trumpets and trombones. For the choreography, she turned to Willie Covan, the black tap dancer who had been made head dance instructor MGM on Eleanor Powell's insistence, after a dazzling career in vaudeville. In Berkeley's most famous film, *42nd Street*, the dancing star, Ruby Keeler, a former nightclub speciality dancer, did her own tap choreography.

Berkeley's approach, however innovative in its time, was completely unacceptable to Kelly, who was trying to combine the roles of performer, choreographer and director, rather than conceiving the numbers as visual spectacles into which the dancers had to fit as best they could, making use of whatever choreographic help they could find for themselves. Kelly, of course, was able to help himself, but at the preview of *For Me and My Gal* he realised he would have to rethink his attitude to dance if he was to achieve the effect he wanted on film. He learned a number of lessons. First, that movement on film is always movement in relation to the camera and that the visual effect of looking through the camera eye at a screen is different from that of looking through the human eye at a stage. Spatial context and scale appear very different – people far away really look tiny – and the effect of movement is also different, favouring especially movement towards the camera. Lateral movements can cancel each other out, unless they are carefully planned. Second, that, as he had concluded from his stage performances, 'whoever or whatever you're portraying, you have to remain totally in character when you dance.'[7] Even more than in the theatre, the dance had to express the dancer's dramatic role, rather than break completely away from it as if it were an isolated performance.

Stanley Donen had been a dancer in the chorus in *Pal Joey* and Kelly asked him to help with his subsequent stage performances and then, in 1942, to come out to Hollywood as his assistant, eventually becoming co-director with him. Donen explains their working procedure in *Cover Girl*, the first film where Kelly had a contractual right to guide his own dance sequences:

> We tried to come up with something novel for him to do. We then developed the idea of the sequence, arranged the transitions in and out [i.e. the timing and framing of cuts from one shot to another, keeping continuity], and mapped out the camerawork and lighting. Very rarely did I tell him about dance steps. We next arranged the music in such a way that it would help to organise the staging and camera movement. During the actual filming Gene worked in front of the camera, I behind. There was no director on the set except us. Then we checked to see if it was photographed properly and supervised the editing. A curious thing about the photographing and editing in those days was that you never shot more than exactly what ended up on the screen [a discipline that surely resulted from planning the sequence precisely around the transitions in the dance as they corresponded to synchronised match cuts in the film].[8]

The big solo number in *Cover Girl*, shot by Kelly and Donen, was the celebrated 'Alter Ego' dance, in which Kelly danced with his own reflection, which steps out of a shop window into the street. As Donen later pointed out, a dance sequence like this was really ahead of what was happening on Broadway. (*Cover Girl* was released in the same year as the stage show *Oklahoma!* and the year before *On the Town*.) Donen rightly points to the influence of Astaire as making this possible. The 'Alter Ego' sequence would not have been possible, for instance, without the precedent of Astaire's 'Bojangles' sequence in *Swing Time*, in which Astaire dances with three of his shadows, an idea suggested by his choreographer, Hermes Pan. As Donen points out, Astaire's numbers often 'owed nothing to the theatre: they were specifically cinematographic'.[9] In fact, from his very first film appearance in *Flying Down to Rio*, Astaire and Pan had insisted on filming him in long takes and wide frame, with match cutting. Indeed, Astaire's understatement fits perfectly into the film format, minimising effort and working through nuance. Kelly, who was much more emphatic and athletic, had

Gene Kelly in the 'Singin' in the Rain' number

to devise a style with more pronounced camera movements, to match the kinetic energy of the camera with that of his body.

The 'Singin' in the Rain' sequence consists simply of ten shots, beginning and ending with a dissolve, lasting in all a little under five minutes. The first is a transition shot, beginning with Don and Kathy kissing on her porch, followed by a brief scene-setting snatch of dialogue, and then another kiss, Kathy leaving and closing the front-door behind her and Don turning into the cut. In the second shot, the first strains of the melody begin to be heard as Don steps down from the porch and, in one gesture, feels the rain with his hand and waves the waiting car away. He saunters cheerily down the sidewalk to an introductory vamp, singing a kind of half-hummed doo-de-doo-de-do-doo-de-do, as suggested by his arranger, Roger Edens. The camera moves with him throughout the shot, then comes in close for the cut.

The song proper begins directly with the third shot. His jaunty stroll becomes more exaggerated and ends with a wild leap up on to a lamp-post. This is Kelly in his acrobatic, Douglas Fairbanks mode. There is the first sound tap as he leaps down again and the camera comes in to close-up as he hugs the lamp-post – 'I'm ready for love ...' – with a huge Kelly grin. He carries on strolling in the fourth shot, which is shorter and more of an interlude, enlivened by a couple of passers-by hurrying along under a sodden newspaper, who do a 180-degree turn wondering at Kelly's antics – his umbrella down in the pouring rain. Again the camera cranes in for the cut, looking down as he looks up, standing with his legs wide apart and arms outstretched, in a 'big' pose, singing and miming, 'I've a smile on my face.'

The fifth shot begins – 'I walk down the lane' – with the squelchy sound effect of walking in the rain making an impact for the first time. He is still singing when he reaches the front of a pharmacy with a gaily decorated window. Here the sidewalk becomes a stage and the dance number begins. The singing dwindles away – just 'Dancing in the rain ...' and scat-like nonsense sounds. The dance, however, is complete with sound taps, and complicated by business with the umbrella, first as a dancing partner, then a juggling prop, and finally a ukulele (the original song, 'Singin' in the Rain' was first introduced on film in 1929 by a ukulele player). Kelly ends the song with the adapted line, 'I'm singin' and dancin' in the rain.'

This last line of the song serves, as Kelly puts it, to 'state the thesis' of the dance which is to follow. 'Unless you're in a ballet, you can't just begin to dance. You have to state your "thesis" in a song first, and then go into the dance. Take the number "Singin' in the Rain". I tell the audience in a song what I'm going to do, and then I do it.'[10] In *Cover Girl*, there is an analogous (though emotionally contrasted) number, the 'Alter Ego' dance, where Kelly has been jilted by the Rita Hayworth character and wanders out into the street, depressed and alone. There he 'states his thesis' with a few phrases of voice-over, as if they were 'stream of consciousness', before going into the dance. Perhaps the bow to the painted figure of a woman in the pharmacy window in 'Singin' in the Rain' is also a nod towards Kelly's shop window reflection in the 'Alter Ego' sequence.

In the sixth shot, the dance proper begins and there is no more singing. At first, there is a clowning feel to the dance, with Kelly hunching his shoulders up, keeping his knees at an awkward angle and juggling with the umbrella again, swinging it round and kicking it up and catching it. This shot ends with a pronounced sound effect, as Kelly runs the metal tip of the umbrella along some railings, like a riveting-machine tap, and the camera comes in again to a cut into and out from the umbrella held up in front of his face. The seventh shot travels with Kelly again as he continues dancing further along the sidewalk to a bookshop and milliner's, with a waterspout gushing water down on to the sidewalk. In this shot the dance becomes less clownish, initially at least, with Kelly backing away from the spout at first, before finally spinning the umbrella again, throwing it high up in the air and catching it, at last ending up under the spout, getting wetter and wetter but cheerier and cheerier.

The dance is now becoming exhibitionist again, in preparation for what is to follow. There is a slightly awkward cut into the eighth shot, again from the umbrella, with an abrupt change in the scale of the frame as Kelly dances off the sidewalk into the street and the camera cranes high up, looking down on the whole street as he traces a circle back to the kerb. As he spins round and round in jubilation, like a whirling dervish, he holds his umbrella stretched fully out with both hands, wide-open again and pitched down in front of him, almost scraping the pavement. As the camera and Kelly come back in to the kerb, there is a match cut leading straight into the ninth shot and the culmination of the dance. This begins with a hopping one-foot-up, one-foot-down movement along the kerb, then a pantomimed tightrope walk along the edge, followed by heavy splashing on the sidewalk, with Kelly kicking and stamping in the prepared puddles and then jumping into the shallow, water-filled pit in the road, with exuberant sounds as he stomps and sploshes water around wildly, but still rhythmically, in an uninhibited frenzy of childishness. After about half a minute, the cop comes into frame and Kelly stops dead, freezes, and then turns and steps back sheepishly on to the sidewalk. He has not done anything really wrong, but the cop acts as a censor who has caught him in the act, bringing his infantile behaviour to an abrupt halt.

The final cut takes us to an over-the-shoulder shot from the cop's point of view as Kelly looks sheepish, with a nervous smile, before a reprise of the last line of the song, by way of explanation, 'I'm dancing and singing in the rain.' Then the camera pulls up high again as Kelly turns and walks off down the street. He hands his umbrella to a soaking passer-by, in a last gesture of cocky defiance of sensible behaviour, waves to the cop and leaves the frame as the shot dissolves into the next sequence. Throughout the five minutes, the camera has been moving almost incessantly to keep up with Kelly's progress, adjusting to his movements as he pantomimes and dances in one location and then travelling on with him to the next, pulling back and up for the most athletic and exuberant moments and moving into close-up for the cuts. The sequences themselves mark clear divisions within the song and in the dance, which are thus segmented into distinct episodes, given continuity by Kelly's ceaseless activity and movement which are interrupted only by brief holds at the cut and by the final dramatic freeze that concludes the dance.

The structure of the piece is one of escalation in the dynamics of movement, as it progresses from the initial still moment on the porch, through the saunter and the vamp, to the song itself, inaugurated first by an acrobatic leap, then falling back to a stroll, and eventually building again into the dance. The dance too becomes increasingly athletic and vigorous, ending with the whirling dance and the wild stomping and splashing, to conclude suddenly with a freeze and a quiet coda as Kelly exits. The movement in the sound is from dialogue to wordless singing along to the vamp and then the song itself, with the lyrics. Shot five functions as the transition into the dance, and the song ends, leaving dance music and tap, which builds in prominence and volume before there is a final reminder of the song and mood music to end.

The sequence is an outstanding example of the use of transitions for the dramatic integration of song and dance numbers into the narrative of the film. It is placed at the most appropriate point in the action, so that Kelly can stay in character as he moves into the dance, which has a long introduction and moves step by step from level to level, shot by shot. He states his thesis and then expresses his joy at falling in love and solving his professional problems simultaneously, in a context which provides emphasis through contrast. Kelly's familiar clown and Fairbanks personae are supportive of the mood, rather than extraneous elements of his performance style. He takes care to use elements of the setting for the dance, with his umbrella going through a series of metamorphoses as a prop, and his dance integrating elements of the street furniture into its structure, as well as making use of the rain and the puddles for sound effects, novelty dancing and dramatic expression. The set itself is also colour-coded in blue and orange tones, with the occasional contrasting red of a municipal fire alarm and the green of a shrubbery. The street lamp and the store windows add sources of light in the darkness.

Above all, however, it is the careful articulation of music, song lyrics, gesture and pantomime, dance and tap, which ensures the success of the piece. Here a major role, together with Kelly and Donen, was played by Roger Edens, the musical arranger. Edens was originally a jazz musician, playing with the Red Nichols Orchestra, alongside Nichols, the Dorsey Brothers, Gene Krupa, Jack Teagarden, Glenn Miller and Harry James. From there, he became vocal arranger for Ethel Merman, went out to Hollywood with her in the 30s, and was hired by Freed in 1934 on the strength of his vocal arrangements for a singer Freed was auditioning, eventually becoming head of the music department at the Freed Unit. A number as complex as 'Singin' in the Rain' does not involve simply dancing to a pre-given score. The song is the starting point, but, as material, it is malleable rather than rigid. The choreographer works out the main elements of the dance number which develops from a score, then plans how to divide it up into episodes for the camera, so that it makes sense in relation to the lyrics, with precisely controlled transitions around the cuts; and then somebody – in this case, Roger Edens – must arrange the music to synchronise with the dancer's steps and rhythms and the camera's movements and cuts.

A number such as 'Singin' in the Rain' required a great solo performer, but also an ability to integrate the solo, both diachronically into the dramatic action of the film and synchronically with the work of the choreographer (in this case the same person, working with Donen and his dance assistant, Carol Haney), the visual director (Stanley Donen, working in close collaboration with Kelly) and the musical arranger (Roger Edens). The original song, by Freed and Brown, was the precondition for the solo, as, more indirectly, was the Comden and Green script which provided its context. Beyond that, Harold Rosson, the cinematographer, had to solve the technical problems created by the rain, by reflecting surfaces, by complex camera movements and crane shots, and by the precisely synchronised timing of those movements.

This complex collaboration is sometimes taken as refuting the *auteur* theory, the thesis that films can be interpreted as structures whose consistency of style and theme derives from a single *auteur*. Yet it is clear that 'Singin' in the Rain' is a summation of Gene Kelly's own work up to that point, echoing and developing numbers he had done in earlier films, crystallising the principles and ideas about dance and film which he had been forming, consciously or unconsciously, since early childhood, more intensely still since his arrival in Hollywood. This is not to deny the crucial role played by his collaborators. *Auteur* structures can be superimposed in the same film and, though Kelly's 'presence' may be the most prominent, this certainly does not mean that we should overlook the contribution of others. 'Singin' in the Rain' can be seen in terms of Donen's career too, and indeed that of Edens, but, in any one instance, there is an implicit hierarchy among *auteurs* and, in the end, a threshold below which individual input becomes increasingly difficult to distinguish and single out.

2

Arthur Freed was a lyrics writer and Nacio Herb Brown a song composer. Together they wrote the original song 'Singin' in the Rain' for the *Hollywood Music Box Revue* of 1927. This was a Los Angeles stage revue modelled on the annual series organised in New York by songwriter Irving Berlin and producer Sam Harris, in competition with the Ziegfeld Follies and George White's Scandals, bringing the public a programme of comedians, singers and showgirls displayed in sumptuous and spectacular sets. Freed and Brown had been working together on and off since they first met in 1921. They had enjoyed two big hits, 'When Buddha Smiles' and 'Take Me in Your Arms', both presented and recorded by the Paul Whiteman band, then the premier white American jazz band, for which Brown had already worked with another collaborator. The year they wrote 'Singin' in the Rain', Brown had another enormous success with a novelty piano rag, 'Doll Dance', which was written in the unusual key of D major, and also featured in the same *Music Box Revue*. There was an enduring vogue for these novelty rags, which featured technically difficult fingering and complicated rhythms, first introduced by Zez Confrey's 'Kitten on the Keys' in 1921; and Brown went on to write another, 'Rag Doll', in 1928, and a third, 'Wedding of the Painted Doll', in 1929, this time with lyrics by Freed.

Following the enormous success of Warner Brothers' sound picture *The Jazz Singer* in the 1927–8 season, the other Hollywood studios all followed suit and began to switch over, first to films with musical soundtracks and shortly afterwards to all-talking pictures. In 1929 MGM's most powerful producer, Irving Thalberg, called in Freed and Brown, on the recommendation of a friend, to discuss his plans for making MGM's first all-talking musical film. Both Brown and Freed were already connected with the film industry. Indeed, like Cosmo in *Singin' in the Rain*, Freed was employed as a mood-music pianist, playing on the set during the production of silent films. Tipped off by their mutual friend, they went to see Thalberg with three new songs ready to show him: 'The Wedding of the Painted Doll', 'You Were Meant for Me', and 'The Broadway Melody'. Thalberg was pleased and, after an audition, the Freed–Brown team was chosen to write the music for MGM's *The*

Broadway Melody, which was premiered triumphantly later in 1929 and became the first of an annual cycle of *Broadway Melody* pictures which ran through the 30s. Freed and Brown stayed on to become regular songwriters for MGM, and Freed, eventually, a producer. The same year, their 'Singin' in the Rain' was featured in *Hollywood Revue of 1929*, the first of many renditions in a series of MGM pictures. Twenty years later, in March 1949, MGM bought out the team's songwriting interests, and their backlist or 'catalogue', including 'Singin' in the Rain', became MGM property. By now Freed had his own production unit at MGM.

'Catalogue' pictures were an established production sub-genre of the musical film, often realised in the form of bio-pics of composers' lives. The month that the Freed–Brown catalogue was sold to MGM, twenty years after he was called in to see Thalberg, Freed announced a forthcoming picture, titled *Singin' in the Rain*, to be made around the Freed–Brown songs. At first he thought of it as a backstage musical, a remake of an old film called *Excess Baggage* (1928), set in vaudeville. It would star the 'machine-gun' tap dancer, Ann Miller, currently appearing in Freed's production of *On the Town*, directed by Gene Kelly and Stanley Donen, which had just started shooting. However, the project lay dormant for a while and was not revived until two years later, in 1950, when Freed was planning *An American in Paris*, starring Gene Kelly, with a script written by Alan Jay Lerner. Lerner had been hired to concoct a coherent story threading together a medley of songs from the Gershwin catalogue. Shortly before *An American in Paris* went into production, Freed hired Betty Comden and Adolph Green, the writers of *On the Town* (who had known Kelly since the summer of 1939, when they worked together in summer stock), to do much the same thing and invent a story for the Freed–Brown catalogue. They arrived in Hollywood from New York in late May 1950.

At first Comden and Green sat and listened to songs from the catalogue, played and sung for them by Roger Edens, Freed's trusted aide and associate producer. It took them some time, a desperate month and a half at least, to decide which songs would fit best and to devise a story which would make sense of the selection. The breakthrough came when they decided to write a script set in Hollywood itself at the time of the change-over to sound, precisely where the Freed–Brown catalogue began. With Stanley Donen, who was available while Gene Kelly finished work on *An American in Paris*, they next embarked on watching old movies from the period, throwing around ideas, stalling and re-starting, until at last they got the structure of the storyline straightened out and wrote the script in a comparatively brief burst of creative energy. The final draft was dated 10 August 1950, and, after some minor revisions, they returned to New York that October.

Kelly did not complete his work on *An American in Paris* until January 1951, after which the pace of events speeded up considerably. By the end of March, *Singin' in the Rain* was already in pre-production and filming began on 18 June. However, Kelly's arrival, combined with casting decisions, brought about major changes both in the selection of songs and in the structure of the script. Whereas it seems that Freed, as the songwriter as well as the producer, had naturally come to see the film as centred on singing, Kelly saw it as based round dancing. The balance changed decisively when the role of Kelly's sidekick was given, not to the pianist and musician Oscar Levant, but, on Kelly's insistence, to the ex-vaudeville hoofer, Donald O'Connor. The starring female role went to Debbie Reynolds, whom the studio wanted to build up into a major star, and who had no particular talent as a singer and no experience at all as a dancer. 'In my opinion,' she said later, 'I was being thrown to the lions.'[11] She was, however, athletic – she had planned to teach gymnastics before she was discovered at a beauty contest in Burbank – and a hard worker. As Kelly put it, she was 'as strong as an ox' and 'a good copyist', who proved able to master the basics of dancing and put in long hours of demanding physical effort at the 'university of hard work and pain'.[12]

O'Connor's arrival meant that Kelly started looking at the Freed–Brown catalogue yet again, this time trying to figure out which songs could best be turned into dance numbers. In fact, two entirely new songs were written. The first, 'Make 'em Laugh', was shamelessly based on Cole Porter's 'Be a Clown', which had been written, also at Kelly's request, for a 1948 Freed picture, *The Pirate*. O'Connor and Kelly, who was choreographer as well as co-director and star (acting, singing and dancing), devised a comedy acrobatic routine which, once seen, never leaves the memory. O'Connor came from a circus family. His father was an acrobat for Ringling Brothers and his mother a tightrope walker

Donald O'Connor in 'Make 'em Laugh'

and bareback rider. By the time O'Connor was born, the family had moved on to vaudeville, where they had an act incorporating circus stunts with more traditional singing and tap dancing. He was on stage, he claims, by the time he was three days old, lying on the piano bench alongside his mother, who had been relegated to piano playing from dancing while she recovered from the birth.

'Make 'em Laugh' was created because Kelly felt that there should be a solo for O'Connor. As O'Connor notes, 'Gene didn't have a clue as to the kind of number it was meant to be.' The two of them went to the rehearsal room and brainstormed and tried things out before finally coming up with what was basically 'a compendium of gags and "shtick" I'd done for years – in fact, going right back to my vaudeville days. Every time I got a new idea or remembered something that had worked well for me in the past, Gene wrote it down and, bit by bit, the entire number was constructed.'[13] The final sequence works because O'Connor succeeded in combining an acrobatic act with a clown act, in the Kelly context of a character dance in a dramatic context. There have been more spectacular acrobatic dance acts – one of the Nicholas Brothers could do two steps up a wall, a backflip, land in the splits and get up again to continue the dance – but O'Connor's number is both spectacular and full of gags, even using the climactic 'up the wall' sequence as lead-in to a final gag as he walks up two walls, crashes through the third (there is a cut after the second) and then picks himself up off-screen and re-emerges, still in the same shot, through the ripped-up plaster. (O'Connor had done the gag years before in vaudeville. To give himself confidence, he had his brother over to rehearse him with a rope.) Kelly stitches the number into the rest of O'Connor's performance, as he also does with the other new song and dance number, 'Moses Supposes' (newly written by Comden and Green, rather than Freed and Brown), by featuring O'Connor's face-pulling (or 'gurning'), which is also used to fill out O'Connor's role as a wag during dialogue scenes.

Finally, Kelly was determined to do a big production number with ballet, as he had for Minnelli in *An American in Paris*, but this time directing it himself in his own film. There were three background preconditions for this decision. First, there was the rise of ballet within the Broadway musical. This occurred in two stages. First, a series of

Rodgers and Hart musicals were produced featuring ballets, beginning with *On Your Toes* in 1936, which was set backstage in the ballet world and for which George Balanchine devised two special ballet numbers, one a light pastiche of *Scheherazade* and the second, a jazz ballet, *Slaughter on Tenth Avenue*, danced by Tamara Geva, from ballet, and Ray Bolger, from tap. This was superficially woven into the action, as a ballet dancer is mistaken for a gangster in a plot twist, and the gangster ballet becomes confused with the gangster story. This was followed the next year by *Babes in Arms*, which featured a dream ballet, 'Peter's Dream', also with Geva, as well as the Nicholas Brothers, choreographed by Balanchine (on the basis of his visits to watch them at the Cotton Club in Harlem)! The dream ballet became the favoured form for integrating ballet numbers into stage musicals, both by relating them to the plot situation and psychology of the dreamer and, at the same time, moving out of the diegetic world of the drama into another and totally fantastic realm.

The real breakthrough came in 1943 with the triumph of *Oklahoma!*, in which Agnes De Mille brought ballet wholesale on to the Broadway stage. In the following year twelve out of the twenty-one musicals produced on Broadway had some kind of ballet number, and 'during the next three and a half years, forty-six included ballet, and twenty-one offered dream ballets, some of staggering ineptitude'.[14] The war years were the time when both ballet and psychoanalysis made their greatest impact on Broadway. The Kurt Weill and Ira Gershwin musical, *Lady in the Dark* (1941), from a story by Moss Hart, was actually set on a psychoanalyst's couch. Hollywood followed suit in due course. *Lady in the Dark* was made into a film by Mitchell Leisen in 1944, with Ginger Rogers starring and the dream ballet metamorphosed into a dream circus. Alfred Hitchcock's *Spellbound* followed in 1945, and Ben Hecht's weird ballet-cum-psychological-thriller *Spectre of the Rose* in 1946. Surrealism and magic realism invaded the movies at the same time, not only with Dali in *Spellbound*, but also with the amazing films made by Albert Lewin and, at MGM, the 'surrealist ballet' danced by Astaire in Minnelli's 1945 *Yolanda and the Thief*, as Parker Tyler noted in his essay 'Finding Freudism Photogenic'. This was the most extravagantly avant-garde work (within the limits of kitsch) ever produced by the Freed Unit. It was choreographed by Eugene Loring,

The Broadway Ballet in *Singin' in the Rain*

who drew on both Dali and Cocteau's *Beauty and the Beast* for the dream (or nightmare) ballet.

The commercial failure of *Yolanda and the Thief* was a setback to the neo-romantic tendency within the Freed Unit. Astaire crisply observed that 'the whole idea was too much on the fantasy side and it did not do too well.' Minnelli's next musical for the Freed Unit, *The Pirate*, came three years later and, starring Kelly rather than Astaire, had a solid armature of vaudeville influences and Fairbanks athleticism. The 'Pirate Ballet' number is boisterous and acrobatic, ambiguously satirising and, by adding what Kelly calls 'classic form' (i.e. balletic movements and references), paying homage to the swashbuckler. The most memorable performers in the film are the Nicholas Brothers, who give their usual stunning display of dance acrobatics in 'Be a Clown'.

Fayard Nicholas later commented, on the subject of working with Kelly, that 'We had to tone down for him, although he told somebody that I was the only dancer who danced like him', presumably a reference to the style Fayard Nicholas called 'classical tap'.[15] 'When we

Fred Astaire in the 'surrealist' ballet in *Yolanda and the Thief*

tapped, we added a little ballet to it, plus a little eccentric [character comedy], a little flash [acrobatics], and we used our hands a great deal. With style and grace we used the whole body from our heads down to our toes. And that's why we called our type of dancing classical tap. That's what it is – the lacing together of tap, balletic leaps and turns, and dazzling acrobatics.'[16] Like Astaire, whom they also greatly admired, the Nicholas Brothers learned from the great syncopated rhythm dancer John Bubbles and the eccentric dancer Ray Bolger, best known now as the Scarecrow in *The Wizard of Oz*, the founding film of the Freed Unit. While Astaire leaned towards the ballroom dancing and 'class act' side of classical tap, Kelly leaned more towards vaudeville, while developing both the ballet and the 'flash' further than Astaire.

Kelly, however, persisted with ballet in *On the Town* with 'Miss Turnstiles' and 'A Day in New York', using Vera-Ellen, who like himself had begun as a tap dancer and moved up to jazz ballet. For the other dancers in 'A Day in New York', however, he had to use substitute performers, including Carol Haney, in the roles played by

Vera-Ellen and Gene Kelly in a ballet sequence from *On the Town*

non-dancers or tap specialists. Agnes De Mille had also set a precedent for this in the dream ballet in *Oklahoma!*, which moved deeper into classical ballet than the rest of the show's choreography. *On the Town*, of course, had started out as a ballet (Jerome Robbins's *Fancy Free*), but by the time it got to Hollywood via Broadway almost nothing of the original remained. At the Freed Unit, an entirely new score was created by Roger Edens and hardly any of Leonard Bernstein's music was left, except the 'Day in New York' ballet. Kelly insisted on the ballet, against Donen's advice, perhaps because he was determined to find a way of retaining a ballet element in the musical, now against the tide.

The tide turned, however, with the American success of Michael Powell and Emeric Pressburger's *The Red Shoes* in 1949, the same year as *On the Town*. *The Red Shoes* proved that a ballet film with a seventeen-minute ballet sequence, starring Moira Shearer and with Robert Helpmann and Leonid Massine as dancer-choreographers, could be a box-office hit. Michael Powell had long cherished the idea of the 'composed film', ever since he saw *The Robber Symphony*, a comic operetta film made in England in 1936 by the Swiss director Friedrich Feher, which was shot synchronised to pre-recorded music. Powell believed that there was an underlying affinity between the film-maker and the composer: 'Their tempos are very closely related to our cutting tempos, their longueurs and their statements are very similar to ours. Whereas even with a writer as clever and subtle as Emeric, I always had this continual battle with words.'[17] Powell experimented with the idea of the composed film in an extraordinary dialogue-free sequence towards the end of *Black Narcissus*, in which a sexually crazed nun stalks and attacks her Mother Superior, driving her to fall to her death over a Himalayan precipice. The next year he took the idea still further in the wonderful ballet sequence of *The Red Shoes*, a turning point in the history of film dance.

The immediate result of the success of *The Red Shoes* was the production by the Freed Unit of *An American in Paris*, as a direct challenge to the British film, an attempt to outdo it both commercially and artistically. *An American in Paris*, directed by Vincente Minnelli, started production in August 1950, and by the time the rest of the film was finished the ballet was still not devised, even though it had been envisaged throughout as the crowning set-piece of the film – to be seventeen minutes long, just as in *The Red Shoes*. The final push came from the designer, Irene Sharaff, who devised a schema of sets, locations and styles built round the work of a series of French painters. After further discussion with Sharaff and Minnelli, this schema then served as the basis for Kelly's choreography, worked out with Carol Haney, to be danced by Kelly with a *bona fide* ballet dancer, Leslie Caron. Finally the musical director, Saul Chaplin, arranged George Gershwin's 'An American in Paris' score to fit with Kelly's dance ideas. The ballet cost more than a quarter as much again to make as the rest of the film, but since it turned out to be the Freed Unit's biggest-grossing picture yet, the decision to splurge on a ballet for the big production number was abundantly justified.

Consequently, when Kelly started to make his next film, *Singin' in the Rain*, which went into production six months after he came off the set of *An American in Paris*, the opportunity was there for him to do another film ballet, one which would combine elements of *On the Town*

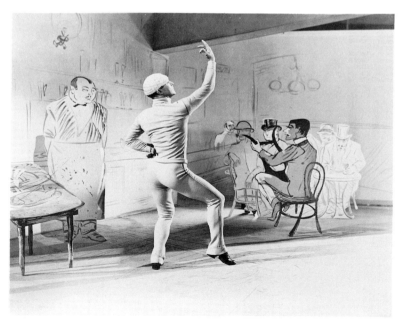

Gene Kelly in the ballet sequence of *An American in Paris*

and *An American in Paris*. This time, however, he had to introduce a dancer for the ballet, since Debbie Reynolds clearly could not be considered. The choice was Cyd Charisse, who had studied ballet in Los Angeles with, among others, Adolph Bolm and Bronislawa Nijinska, and then danced with the Ballets Russes under the name of Siderova. When the war broke up the company, she returned to Los Angeles and was given a dancing role in Gregory Ratoff's *Something to Shout About* by David Lichine, another Ballets Russes dancer who had been hired as choreographer. This brought her to the attention of Robert Alton and soon she was at the Freed Unit, where she became the resident MGM ballet dancer.

For *Singin' in the Rain*, Kelly decided to build his ballet around two of Freed–Brown's classic songs, 'Broadway Melody' and 'Broadway Rhythm', which had been suggested for a big production number by Comden and Green, but set on a recording stage at the studio, in classic 'putting on a show' style. The transformation to ballet meant they had to devise some rationale for the sequence as part of *The Dancing Cavalier* (the film we see being made in *Singin' in the Rain*) and they came up with a solution which would have been completely implausible if it had not been loosely based on *DuBarry Was a Lady*. As explained in the script by Cosmo, 'The hero is a modern young hoofer in a Broadway show. Right? ... Well, one night backstage, he's reading *The Tale of Two Cities* between numbers, see? A sandbag falls on his head, and he dreams he's back during the French Revolution! This way we get in modern dancing numbers – Charleston-Charleston – but in the dream part we can use all the costume stuff – right?'[18] Similarly, in *DuBarry Was a Lady* (Cole Porter, 1939; film version by Roy Del Ruth, 1943), the anti-hero, Louie, a nightclub washroom attendant (hat-check boy in the film), accidentally drinks a Mickey Finn intended for his rival and imagines he has become Louis XV in pursuit of the beautiful Madame DuBarry, with The Black Arrow, played by Gene Kelly, as his rival in the film version.

However, Kelly interpolated yet another sequence, nested inside 'The Broadway Ballet', a scarf dance based around the legend of Isadora Duncan and Loie Fuller, but using an enormous fifty-foot veil of white China silk attached to Charisse's costume. The scarf 'dances' with Charisse and Kelly, its movements choreographed along with theirs, as it flows out behind her, coils around her or flies vertically into the air above her. Kelly thought originally that he could move the veil round with a wind-machine, like the one he uses in 'You Were Meant for Me'. But, because of its size, he ended up having to use aeroplane motors, manipulated in rehearsal by Carol Haney and Jeanne Coyne, counting every bar. 'We had to experiment for days before we discovered that by pointing the machines down on the ground, we could make the veil shoot up, or by pointing them straight at Cyd and lowering the velocity, we could get it to fly back and ruffle slightly.'[19] Charisse remembers that she could hardly keep on her feet because of the pressure of the wind. But the precise choreography of the veil works with the dance, and Kelly at last succeeds in producing a number which vies with its counterpart in *The Red Shoes* and magically transforms stubborn technical ingenuity and immense physical effort into an ethereal dream.

Singin' in the Rain finished production on 21 November 1951. A little over a year and a half later, Gene Kelly was in London at the time

Cyd Charisse

of Queen Elizabeth's Coronation. He was invited by Jules Stein of MCA to watch the procession from his balcony window. It was raining and Kelly and his family had difficulty getting through the crowds to the MCA building.

> Suddenly, over the loudspeaker system, a man who had been keeping everyone informed about what was happening, said: 'Now ladies and gentlemen, I'd like you all to join Gene Kelly in 'Singin' in the Rain' and on came the record. A few seconds later, thousands of lovely, cold, wet, shivering English men and women started to sing. It was the biggest thrill of my life. It beat anything I'd ever known – the opening of *Pal Joey*, my Academy Award – you name it. It was a once-in-a-lifetime experience, and I felt if I never achieved another thing – which was the way things seemed to be going – I'd have justified my existence. Suddenly the English could do no wrong.[20]

Indeed, despite the triumph of *Singin' in the Rain* and the special Academy Award that had come with it, things were not going especially well for Kelly. He had left America for Europe on New Year's Eve, just a few days after the first preview screening of *Singin' in the Rain*, which was on Boxing Day. He arrived in France on New Year's DDay, 1952, and did not return to America until nineteen months later, in the first week of August 1953. Thus he had to cancel his planned starring appearance in a musical version of *Huckleberry Finn*, and missed the Academy Awards which honoured *An American in Paris* and Kelly personally. Instead he made two terrible films in Europe, one in Germany and one, for the Boulting Brothers, in England, and struggled to make his full-scale ballet film, *Invitation to the Dance*, at the MGM studios at Borehamwood. This was Kelly's most personal and most experimental project, but was eventually delayed and not released by an unenthusiastic MGM until 1957; and then, of course, it failed dismally at the box office as well as baffling the critics.

On the record, the explanation for Kelly's departure immediately after making two of the Freed Unit's three most commercially successful films is that he wished to take advantage of new US tax laws which exempted Americans from tax if they stayed abroad for eighteen months. In fact, this did not even work out as planned, because the law was repealed before the period was over and, in the end, Kelly not only stayed in Europe but got no tax benefit from it. Doubtless the timing of Kelly's departure was dictated by the tax law, but it is hard to resist the conclusion that there was another reason for his absence from America, one shared by many other people in Hollywood. 1951 was the year in which the second wave of House Committee on UnAmerican Activities (HUAC) hearings hit Hollywood, inaugurating the 'scoundrel years' of blacklisting, informing, denouncing and desperate pleading of the Fifth Amendment.

Anti-leftism had always existed in Hollywood, of course, simmering away and coming to the boil in periods such as that of Upton Sinclair's 1934 campaign for Governor of California, and again during the Popular Front period at the end of the 30s and into the 40s, when the Washington-based Dies Committee opened fire on Hollywood, with the local Tenney Committee soon following suit. These Committees focused on the Communist Party as their most exposed adversary, but were handicapped, of course, by the wartime alliance with the Soviet Union. It was not until after the defeat of Germany and Japan, and the first stirrings of the Cold War, that the anti-leftist campaign really hit its stride, culminating in 1947 with the subpoena of the 'unfriendly nineteen', eventually reduced to the 'unfriendly ten' who appeared that October before the UnAmerican Activities Committee in Washington and took the Fifth Amendment.

Almost immediately afterwards the Hollywood studio chiefs met in New York and decided to cut the Hollywood Ten adrift and adopt a policy of 'self-regulation' which, they hoped, might head off any further outside interference in their affairs. Thus the basis for a blacklist was established. For the next two and a half years and more the Ten, accused of contempt of Congress, fought to stay out of jail, taking their case to the Supreme Court, which finally refused to hear their cases in April 1950. On 11 June the first two, Howard Lawson and Dalton Trumbo, went to jail, and all but Adrian Scott, whose sentencing was delayed because he was too ill to travel, had joined them by the end of the month. Through the summer there were rumours that a new round of HUAC hearings were about to begin, and early the next year the first subpoenas arrived. Even before this time Hollywood leftists had begun to leave the country, and the stream now gathered speed. On 8 March the Committee hearings began again. The same month *Singin' in the Rain* went into pre-production.

The House Committee was now flanked by an array of vigilante groups which had grown up during the previous years. These groups effectively took control of the industry's 'self-regulation' machinery through public denunciations, secret blacklists and quasi-official clearance procedures. They would name a person, privately or publicly, and then force the blacklisted person to clear themselves by acknowledging their fault, attacking Communism and, in many cases, collaborating with the FBI or the Committee by giving lists of other names to be blacklisted or subpoenaed. The UnAmerican Activities Committee was at the apex of this informal system, empowering it with legal and governmental authority. Between the House Committee and the studios there were two tiers of organisations like, on the one hand, *Red Channels*, the American Legion, the Hearst press and so on, which accumulated, disseminated and published names of potential blacklist victims whom they could threaten with exposure, and, on the other hand, clearance organisations like the Motion Picture Industry Council (run by Roy Brewer, an anti-communist union boss). Often enough, the blacklisting organisations also doubled as clearance organisations. They would bring a case to a studio's attention and then indicate how the 'problem' could be solved.

It is important to stress that although the main brunt of the campaign was borne by Communists and ex-Communists, the aim of those running the blacklist was much wider. In effect, they wanted to break the power of the entire left in Hollywood for good and all. Thus, although they began by pinpointing Communists, they soon extended their attack to members of any Popular Front organisation, to supporters of the Wallace Presidential bid of 1948, to liberals who had opposed the operations of the House Committee on free speech grounds, and so on. In order to do this, it was necessary to link their victims by a chain of evidence to people who were indeed Communists, with whom they had once appeared on the same platform or whose names had appeared on the same list of signatories to a political advertisement, or with whom they had once been close friends or associates. Evidently Communists and ex-Communists were more likely to be called in front of the Committee itself, along with a sprinkling of 'dupes' persuaded or intimidated into believing that their best course was to grovel, recant and inform. These people served as examples for all the others on the left who were forced to live in a climate of anxiety and fear, not knowing whether they had been blacklisted or would be or what they should do if they were.

Gene Kelly was brought up in the steel industry town of Pittsburgh in the midst of the Depression. Politically, he soon came to identify with the left. His biographer, Clive Hirschhorn, writes of 'the socialist principles he had been developing since his college days';[21] and while he was in New York, he mixed in left-wing circles which were quite typical of artists and intellectuals during the Roosevelt years. This was the milieu from which many of the Hollywood left came, moving, like Kelly, from home town to New York to Los Angeles. Indeed, when he arrived in Hollywood, Kelly became much more politically active, for instance in the Screen Actors Guild, the Hollywood actors' union, of which he became First Vice-President. He was on the Executive of the Guild during the bitter Hollywood strikes of 1946, based on demarcation disputes among the studio craft unions, which split left and right as they escalated. Hirschhorn notes that 'during the course of his negotiations [on a union delegation to AFL headquarters in Chicago], he was accused by the right of championing the cause of the strikers', and observes how he had the reputation of a 'free-thinking liberal' with 'anti-Establishment sentiments' who 'a few years later would not have been surprised had he found himself on Senator McCarthy's notoriously destructive blacklist and labelled a Communist.'[22]

In fact, Kelly was indeed harassed for his political views by the Tenney Committee, whose reports of 1947 and 1948 specifically named him, not for his union activities, but for his active role in the Progressive Citizens of America, a pro-Wallace organisation of which he became Vice-Chairman; in the Hollywood Democratic Committee, of which he was Vice-President, which was judged 'a CP front' by the Committee; and in other similar associations. Evidence given to the House Committee in 1947 similarly associated him with the Progressive Citizens of America. Moreover, Kelly actively intervened against the House Committee when it subpoenaed the 'unfriendly nineteen'. He supported the Committee for the First Amendment, which was formed to defend their rights. He was Master of Ceremonies at the mass rally which was called by the Progressive Citizens of America in solidarity with the nineteen. He went on the famous planeload of stars who flew to Washington at the time of the hearings to protest them, although MGM had pleaded with him not to go. All these honourable acts led, of course, to his becoming one of Jack Tenney's 'most frequent targets'.

By 1949, Kelly seems to have decided that it was prudent to give up his political activity. This did not, however, get rid of his problems. The furies of the right had long memories when it came to settling scores. Moreover, Kelly's wife, the actress Betsy Blair, was even more vulnerable than he was. Following Kelly, Blair had in their New York days, as she put it, 'become interested in socialism myself – so much so, in fact, that I even attended some marxist lectures, which Gene didn't. In that area of my life, it was really a case of the pupil following the master.'[23] She became involved in a number of 'Communist front' organisations – the Joint Anti-Fascist Refugee Committee, the Committee to Elect Henry Wallace, and the Hollywood Committee for the Arts, Sciences and Professions, almost the last of such bodies to survive. According to Hirschhorn, she 'for a period, did, in fact, believe in Soviet Communism'.[24] Betsy Blair herself observed that 'most of the studios considered me untouchable and my career definitely suffered. There's no doubt about that.' In fact she was blacklisted. Her last Hollywood role for many years was in Anatole Litvak's *The Snake Pit*, released in 1949, where she gives a striking performance as a mute psychotic. Her next was in Delbert Mann's *Marty* in 1955. To get this role, she was asked, following the normal clearance procedure, to write a letter to the American Legion confessing her errors, naming names and recanting. She refused to do this and Gene Kelly, then in production on *It's Always Fair Weather*, stormed in to see Dore Schary, the head of the studio, and gave him an ultimatum. In Hirschhorn's words: 'Either Schary used his influence to clear Betsy's name, so that she got the part, or he would stop work on *It's Always Fair Weather*. Put like that Schary had little choice, and in Gene's presence he called the American Legion in Washington and personally vouchsafed her good character. She got the part.'[25]

Nor was Kelly the only person involved in *Singin' in the Rain* to be potentially under threat. Betty Comden and Adolph Green had begun their careers in 1938 with a cabaret act called the Revuers working at Max Gordon's Village Vanguard in Greenwich Village, New York, where Gordon had been holding poetry readings but, in his own words, 'began to look for real acts to put in, and what I wanted was something that would comment on the social and political scene.'[26] As a result of a chance meeting with Judy Tuvim, later Judy Holliday, he hired the group organised by Adolph Green, who had met Holliday at a summer camp, and Betty Comden, whom he knew from New York University. They formed the nucleus of the Revuers, along with Alvin Hammer, a comic monologuist, and John Frank, a pianist. The Revuers wrote and performed their own songs, skits and take-offs, including, among the parodies of Hollywood movies and Wagnerian operas, a sketch about the UnAmerican Activities Committee and a spoof of Clifford Odets's *Waiting for Lefty*. In the words of a contemporary left-wing reviewer, 'not as political as TAC [the Theater Arts Committee cabaret] but as satiric about the right things, the show brings celebrities and scouts about town to huzzah and cheer and wonder how Broadway does without them. But it won't be long for as one says in Hoboken – they have *quelque chose sur la boule*.'[27] Sure enough, they eventually made it to Broadway, Comden and Green with *On the Town*, based on the music of Green's old friend Leonard Bernstein, and to Hollywood.

There Alvin Hammer appeared before the UnAmerican Activities Committee on 6 July 1951 and took the Fifth Amendment, thus ending his Hollywood career. Judy Holliday, the founder of the Revuers, appeared before the Senate's MacCarran Committee on 26 March 1952, where like Lucille Ball before her she played the scatty star with no politics and no memory, even though Holliday had apparently sponsored the 1949 Waldorf Conference and the Prague World Youth Festival, appeared on a picket line, defended the Spanish Republic, sent greetings to the Moscow Art Theatre, and so on. She was asked point-blank about Comden and Green: 'Adolph Green and Betty Comden, with whom you were associated in the Revuers, have Communist-front records, do they not?'[28] Holliday refused to believe it and stonewalled through a series of follow-up questions about their supposed activities. The previous month, Adolph Green had been named both as a Communist Party member to the House Committee by Harvey

Matusow (who later admitted perjuring himself in front of the Committee), and as a member of People's Songs, with which Kelly was also associated by the Tenney Committee. People's Songs was an organisation built round artists like Pete Seeger and Woody Guthrie, which supplied songs for the Wallace campaign in a last burst of Popular Front activity.

Whatever the real political allegiance of this group of friends and colleagues, who had all known each other since 1940 and whose careers remain linked in the public memory because of films like *On the Town* and *Singin' in the Rain*, it is clear that, in the words of Malcolm Goldstein, they formed 'a durable part of Popular Front culture'. It is not surprising that when Arthur Freed decided he had to cancel *Huckleberry Finn*, because its two writers, Donald Ogden Stewart and Yip Harburg, had both fallen foul of the blacklist, Gene Kelly too decided it was time to go, first to France and then to London. In Europe, after all, he could still work and Betsy Blair was able to find some parts, thanks to her friendship with Anatole Litvak. Orson Welles, another graduate of the Popular Front who now found himself in Europe, hired her to play Desdemona in his film of *Othello*, though she was soon fired.

When Kelly finally returned to Hollywood, after six months in France and more than a year in Britain, he got his clearance through Roy Brewer, the right-wing trade union boss of IATSE, who had led the AFL fight against the rival CIO in Hollywood, using the full clout of a union renowned for its mafia connections. As John Cogley notes in his *Report on Blacklisting*:

> The dancing star, Gene Kelly, who had been so harassed that he went off to Europe, came home and commended Brewer at a AFL Film Council meeting as having done more for the unity of labor than any one man. Kelly then went on to note 'Irving Brown's program in France in which he is doing an especially fine job of persuading members of French labour unions to the anti-Commie position of the American labour movement [i.e. a lightly coded endorsement of Brewer's efforts to extend the blacklist to exiles working in Europe].' The speech was accepted as a public pronouncement that Kelly's 'list' troubles were over and that he now had Brewer's approval.[29]

Kelly could now continue with his work on *Brigadoon*. His troubles had been acute since December 1951, the month that Dore Schary announced Kelly's imminent departure to the Freed Unit. This was the month when the veteran anti-Communist journalist, 'Doc' Matthews, now working as a columnist for the *American Legion Magazine*, named *Singin' in the Rain* specifically in 'Did the Movies Really Clean House?', a landmark article that challenged the studios to put more enthusiasm into their purge of the left and led directly to the quasi-institutionalising of the blacklist on the American Legion's terms. Nineteen long months passed before the studio and Kelly were able to work out an acceptable clearance.

It is tempting to try to interpret *Singin' in the Rain* in terms of the political climate in which it was made: to note, for example, that the story hinges on the thwarting of a plot to blacklist Kathy Selden, launched by an informer and enforced by using the media to pressure a weak-willed studio, which ultimately puts profit before principle, until finally the situation is resolved and virtue triumphs in a wishful happy ending. Or perhaps the 'Singin' in the Rain' dance sequence represents Kelly's determination to be optimistic in a miserable political climate, insisting that he may have behaved in an unorthodox, uninhibited way, but that basically he is joyous and generous and American whatever the law may think as it holds him in its disapproving gaze. Perhaps.

The tragedy remains that Hollywood allowed itself to be intimidated into losing so much of its talent or, in the end, only kept it at the price of humiliating conformity and compromise which enervated and destroyed its creative energy, right through to the 1960s. The depth of this tragedy is still not recognised to its full extent. It is still necessary to insist on how devastating the right-wing roll-back of the post-war decade was. *Singin' in the Rain* was the peak of Kelly's achievement and that of his collaborators. There are many reasons why it was never surpassed. The studios were divorced from the theatres, cinema itself gave way to television, Tin Pan Alley gave way to rock'n'roll, and in all three cases Hollywood was painfully uncertain how to respond. But, as well as these institutional, cultural and technological trends, I believe that it was McCarthyism, in the broad sense of the term – the determination to destroy all traces of Popular Front culture – that first tragically limited the MGM musical and eventually brought it to a halt. In this light, it is somehow appropriate that the Freed Unit's last productions, in 1959, should have been *The Subterraneans* and *The Bells Are Ringing*, the last, heroic stand of Judy Holliday, Betty Comden and Adolph Green.

3

In the 1962 *Sight and Sound* poll, only one critic named *Singin' in the Rain* in his 'Top Ten List'. In 1972, there were five. In 1982, seventeen listed *Singin' in the Rain* and it now came fourth overall, running immediately ahead of Fellini's *8½*, Eisenstein's *Battleship Potemkin* and Hitchcock's *Vertigo*. What caused this steady ascent? First, it should be noted that during the 70s MGM released *That's Entertainment*, a compendium of clips from MGM musicals which highlighted *Singin' in the Rain* more than any other film except perhaps *The Band Wagon*, and then, shortly afterwards, re-released *Singin' in the Rain* itself. Also, as the veteran editor of *Sight and Sound*, Penelope Houston, observed in her introduction to the 1982 lists, *Singin' in the Rain* had also begun to be revived on television. Availability of films is the first necessary condition for their artistic evaluation.

A second important factor, however, was the steadily growing impact of the re-evaluation of taste which had begun in the 50s and 60s with *auteur* theory. Before this time, the canon of great films was dominated by European masterpieces and, from Hollywood, a handful of pioneering sound films and a very few more recent films with significant social messages. Post-war American films first entered the canon surprisingly late and, at first, on terms laid down by auteurism. Then, as Hollywood films were given new stature through the discovery of *auteurs*, interest began to extend to genre films which were not necessarily made by recognised name directors. The musical was probably the genre intrinsically most resistant to simplistic auteurism, precisely because it was so obviously dependent on collaboration, reflecting its mix of film, drama, music and dance. Nonetheless Minnelli was recognised very early, because of his distinctive visual style, which stretched across genres, allowing critics to integrate his musicals into his *oeuvre*. Kelly and Donen posed more problems because they formed a team in themselves, as co-directors, and because, of the two, only Donen had a significant body of non-musical work. It is interesting that Tony Thomas's *The Films of Gene Kelly* treats Kelly primarily as a performer, whereas Joseph Andrew Casper's *Stanley Donen* treats Donen, of course, as a director. Nonetheless, in the end, the confluence of auteurism, centred on an aesthetic re-evaluation of Hollywood, and a growing interest in the study of popular culture which was more responsive to genre eventually cleared a path for *Singin' in the Rain*.

There was, however, a third factor. *Singin' in the Rain* benefited critically from an increased interest in self-reflexive cinema, in films which themselves deal with the process of film-making. In this respect, it makes sense that the star of *Singin' in the Rain* should rise with Fellini's *8½*, however different the films are in other respects. European films like *8½*, Fellini's fantasy cinematic autobiography, or Truffaut's *Day for Night*, said to be influenced by *Singin' in the Rain*, or Wajda's *Everything for Sale* or Wenders's *Kings of the Road* or Godard's *Passion* have inevitably led to a renewed interest in 'Hollywood-on-Hollywood' as a subgenre. Indeed, in general terms, this could almost be seen as a symptom of the impact of post-modernism on both film-making and film criticism, the fascination with the foregrounding of conventionally concealed technology, and the development of an aesthetic which welcomed recycling and *mise en abîme*. *Singin' in the Rain*, moreover, deals with a particularly crucial moment in film history, the coming of sound. As well as a surface of retro pastiche and affectionate parody, it also has a thematic core which raises questions about the relation of sound and image, authenticity and unauthenticity, and so on, however lavishly coated with songs, jokes and bravura wit.

The reflexivity of *Singin' in the Rain* derives, in the first instance, from its status as a 'backstage musical', in which, instead of putting on a play in a barn, as Judy Garland and Mickey Rooney did in their cycle of films for the Freed Unit, the protagonists are making a movie. For Comden and Green this was an opportunity for stringing together a series of skits or spoofs of a kind they had specialised in since their Revuers days. These skits, however, were based on genuine love and knowledge. As Gary Carey notes, writing about the Revuers, 'Since they were addicted to the absurdities they ridiculed, there was always a core of affection beneath their sketches.'[30] Comden and Green were *cinéphiles*, or even cultists, bordering on camp. Green, in particular, was a maestro of 'trivial erudition', who loved to play at quoting the first and last lines of a movie and challenging his partners to identify the source. He loved obscure bit players and could recognise them in walk-on parts. He had to be reminded that not everybody knew who Rafaela Ottiano was. It was the same with music. When he first met Leonard Bernstein, they 'immediately recognised each other as kindred souls when they discovered that they could each identify a Prokofiev symphony after hearing the opening three measures.'

When Comden and Green arrived on the MGM lot to write *Singin' in the Rain*, they discovered, of course, that a large number of people there, from Arthur Freed down, remembered the coming of sound well. To Comden and Green it was already the glorious imaginary past, but at MGM it was people's lives. The film-makers could grill people on their memories and search for relics of those so recent, long-gone days in the props store and in forgotten corners of the lot. As Kelly put it, 'Almost everything in *Singin' in the Rain* springs from the truth. It's a conglomeration of bits of movie lore.'[31] Veterans on the set still remembered the early problems of sound recording; the art directors unearthed equipment from the past and manufactured Cooper-Hewitt lights and an 'icebox' to house the sound camera from old specifications and designs; a neglected glass sound-stage was found and brought back into service; the furniture from *Flesh and the Devil*, starring John Gilbert and Greta Garbo in 1927, was rediscovered and used in Don Lockwood's home; the costume designer, Walter Plunkett, devised costumes for Lina Lamont which were 'as nearly as I can remember, duplicates of some I did in all seriousness for Lilyan Tashman. And she was the epitome of chic at that time.'[32] Detail and loving care gave *Singin' in the Rain* a depth which is belied by its surface frothiness.

In its narrative line, the script was more complex than most backstagers. First, it has a fairy-tale foundation. The kernel of its story is basically a variant on that of Hans Christian Andersen's *The Little Mermaid*, plus a trick and counter-trick, and coupled with a typical romance plot consisting of a series of real and threatened separations and reunions between a couple. The heroine has her voice taken from her by a wicked witch and cannot marry the hero unless it has been recovered. At the end, like Cinderella, she is transfigured into a fairy-tale princess (a star), so that she can marry her prince. In fact, *Singin' in the Rain* combines all three sub-genres of the musical noted by Rick Altman in his magisterial analysis of the genre: the Show Musical, the Fairy-Tale Musical, and the Folk Musical. As he puts it, 'The show musical involves the spectator in the creation of a work of art; the fairy tale musical creates a utopian world like that of the spectator's dreams; the folk musical projects the spectator into a mythicised version of the cultural past.'[33] In other words, Hollywood functions as a place for creating a show, as a magic kingdom, and as a site of Americana, coloured by 'the transforming power of memory'. Similarly, the film combines in one the three typical locations of these sub-genres: the studio as backstage, culminating in a triumphant mastery of both art and technology; the studio as distant goal and imaginary dream-world, culminating in a successful romance and a joyous partnership; and the studio as happy family, threatened by disruption but finally coming together into an exclusive and closely bonded unit.

The disruption of the studio family and, more specifically, the professional couple, Don Lockwood and Kathy Selden, is threatened of course through the appropriation of Kathy's voice by Don's silent film partner, Lina Lamont. Here Comden and Green, and Kelly, once again drew on the Revuers. Lina's voice in the film is modelled on the voice used by Judy Holliday in her first big post-Revuers success, *Born Yesterday* (1950), and Jean Hagen, who plays the part, was actually Holliday's replacement in the original stage production when it went on tour. Lina has to be exposed as the deceptive possessor of the voice, and its real owner, Kathy, can then replace her as Don's sound film partner.

Thus the core issue in the film is that of the relationship between sound and image. Things can only end happily when, so to speak, a properly 'married print' is produced, in which voice and image are naturally joined together. The underlying theme is that of nature as truth and unity, versus artifice as falsehood and separation. Kathy's voice becomes a kind of ornament which can be subtracted from her and added to Lina in defiance of its natural origins. This privileging of the bond between essence, body and voice, as the *logos* on which truth must be founded, is precisely that which was later to be attacked by the philosopher Jacques Derrida as the illusory basis of all Western metaphysics, from the time of the Greeks on. He associates this theory of the *logos*, normalised philosophically to the point where it is scarcely noticed, with the persistent philosophical denigration of writing as a form of artifice, obeying the logic of a supplement or additional ornament, rather than an integral reality. Read in this way, *Singin' in the Rain* could be characterised as the purest example of the translation of such a metaphysics from the realm of language to that of cinema. Dubbing, here, represents the cinematic form of writing, through which sound is separated from its origin and becomes a potentially free-floating, and thus radically unreliable, semantic element.

The inevitable culmination of *Singin' in the Rain* has then to be an unveiling, which rolls back the grammatological curtain and reveals what must be, metaphorically, the naked truth: the *logos* made spectacle, for which Don Lockwood has been waiting so long in order that his romance should finally be consummated. It remains an endearing irony that, in reality, if I can so use the phrase, Debbie Reynolds's singing voice in the film was in fact dubbed by Jean Hagen, so that what we see and hear is the unveiling of a mystery which subverts its own appearance of authenticity. As Debbie Reynolds put it, 'Jean's real voice, however, was lovely and she dubbed herself.' It seems that, after all, the ear is more easily ensnared than the eye. Although, to tell the truth, to deceive the ear, deception of the eye is necessary too. In Debbie Reynolds's words, once more, 'I thought I was good at lip-synching until we went before the camera. Then the pressure was like nothing I'd ever known. Putting the song together with the dancing takes a very special precision. They had one man on the set who did nothing but watch our lips. If there was one mistake, it was "CUT!" and we'd have to start all over again.'[34]

Thematically, it is important that the site of deception is the image of the woman, rather than the man. In ideological terms, in our culture, it is woman who is primarily taken to represent 'nature', and therefore unnatural deception by a woman, such as Lina, can be construed as all the more reprehensible. Yet there is an ambivalence at work. Whereas, on the one hand, for Kathy to be a star, her natural voice must prevail, on the other hand, in the 'You Were Meant for Me' number, set on the sound stage, Kathy is made into a star by being artificially beautified. Stage lighting creates sunset and 'mist from the distant mountain'. Five hundred thousand kilowatts from a large spotlight creates a moon up above and, finally, a wind machine produces 'a soft, summer breeze'.[35] Here woman is placed on the side of fantasy rather than nature, and fantasy requires artifice. Here the technology of cinema is used to create the romantic setting which allows Don to confess his love, the traditional product of the dream factory.

Dance, on the other hand, which is Kelly's own province, must be shown as unfaked, through the use of long takes and wide frames. (The movements at least must be for real. Taps can be dubbed, as Hermes Pan dubbed those of Ginger Rogers dancing with Fred Astaire.) Hence the demand on Debbie Reynolds to master the basics of dancing, because as long as she was in shot with Kelly she had to be genuinely performing. In music videos, on the other hand, or in a film like *Flashdance*, the dancing can be faked by segmenting and editing, so that the feet do not belong to the dancer or the movements are so abbreviated that the dance is effectively created in the montage. For Kelly, obsessed with the validity of male dance, the presence of the body was all-important, a male body that is acceptably exhibitionist in its athleticism. In his 1956 television programme *Dancing: A Man's Game*, Kelly juxtaposed male dancers with sportsmen, like the boxer Sugar Ray Robinson. In his films, it is the male body which is the primary object of the spectator's gaze, and this role as passive target of the spectator's look is validated by the hyper-active demonstration of masculine qualities, most familiar as spectacle in sports. Thus in *Singin' in the Rain*, the female body needs to be romanticised and beautified by the man, whereas his own body is naturally the focus of attention. Her natural charms lie in her mellifluous voice, which is metaphorically related, I would argue, to the soul rather than to the body, whereas his are objectified in physical activity. Thus the married print, like the married couple, is the marriage of voice with image, woman with man, soul with body.

The quest for cinematic authenticity goes even further. Kelly was rightly proud of shooting *On the Town* in New York itself, on location in the streets and on the waterfront. He insisted, against the wishes of the studio, that even a musical would benefit from being shot on location. Thus *On the Town* followed in the wake of De Sica's *Bicycle Thieves* or

Hellinger's *Naked City*. At the same time, of course, New York was 'cinematised' through framing and lighting and Technicolor. *Singin' in the Rain* was also, in a paradoxical sense, shot on location. The story is set in a film studio, and thus when we see a set, it is an authentic set. The artificial pastness of the set is reduced as far as possible by antiquarian exactitude, which gives an effect of authenticity. Part of the effect of the film comes from this oscillation between artifice and reality, between the fake studio and the real studio, the fake antique and the real antique, which runs through the film.

As with location shooting, Kelly's interest in the 'integrated drama' also represents another form of the quest for authenticity, in the sense of a rejection of the 'supplement'. The insistence on 'integration' springs from a feeling that there is something artificial about musical comedy when it includes numbers ornamentally, as interludes of gorgeous spectacle, without making them seem to develop naturally from the book or script or dramatic logic of a situation. Yet Kelly's commitment to the 'integrated drama' was far from absolute. Indeed,

The film studio set

Stanley Donen has criticised him for interpolating heterogeneous ballet numbers into both *On the Town* and *Singin' in the Rain*. He comments on the 'A Day in New York' sequence in *On the Town*: 'I felt that the ballet was an interruption to the film's main thrust. I equally felt that the "Broadway Melody–Broadway Rhythm" ballet was an interruption to the main thrust of *Singin' in the Rain*.'[36] In similar terms, Stuart Hall and Paddy Whannel commented in their 1964 book *The Popular Arts* that *Singin' in the Rain* was 'flawed by a rather pretentious ballet sequence'.[37] Although I think they are referring to an unjustified change of register from vernacular dance forms to the elite mode of ballet, the force of the criticism is the same. Either way, there is felt to be a rift in the required homogeneity of the work, and this gives the effect of an unmotivated interruption.

Yet there is an unimpeachable historical precedent for the insertion of numbers which interrupt the 'main thrust' of the dramatic narrative. The storyline of *Singin' in the Rain*, which was originally devised to make some sense of the Freed–Brown song catalogue, rather than falling back on a completely modular revue format, can simply be regarded as 'cartilage', to use the word favoured by the Russian critic, Victor Shklovsky. Shklovsky argued that the 'integrated' word of literature was a historically specific idea, which developed for reasons internal to the evolution of literary form. If we look back far enough, we find works which are basically short story collections, joined together by the 'cartilage' of a framing story: Scheherazade's stay of execution in *The Thousand and One Nights*, escape from the Black Death in *The Decameron*, a pilgrimage to the holy martyr's shrine in *The Canterbury Tales*. Over time the role of the framing story began to grow and its protagonists, from being masters of ceremony or anchor persons, so to speak, began to become the principal subjects of the work, with the emergence of the picaresque novel. Now the embedded material began to be viewed as merely interpolation or digression. Nevertheless, this material remained prominent in many great works: consider, for instance, Cervantes's *Don Quixote*, Sterne's *Tristram Shandy* or Melville's *Moby Dick*. Shklovsky believed that the idea of 'total integration' was specific to the Victorian novel and was bound to be challenged again in the twentieth century, simply in order to renew the form and, through the new principle of montage, introduce a fresh way of looking at the world. Thus *Singin' in the Rain*, based round a song catalogue, takes us back full cycle to Chaucer and Boccaccio.

In the world of theatrical musical comedy, three sub-genres reflected different stages of development towards integration. Revue had a very loose, non-dramatic framing structure; mainstream musical comedy introduced narrative and character, but still treated musical numbers as interludes; operetta strove towards a more integrated form. The *Oklahoma!* revolution was basically an attempt to lift musical comedy up into the sphere of operetta, while retaining American popular music for the score, rather than adopting operetta's sub-classical European style, which derived from Strauss or Lehar. It is significant that there was an implicit hierarchy among these three sub-genres. In *Singin' in the Rain* there is a sequence where the same number is shown as performed in burlesque, vaudeville and revue, becoming less vivacious and more elaborate at each level. A similar scale could be demonstrated with revue, musical comedy and operetta, showing tighter dramatic integration at each level. Musical comedy in the cinema reflected the same distinctions, but without such a pronounced sense of hierarchy.

Gene Kelly's aesthetic, however, was more complex and, although it reflected a drive towards dramatic integration, there was a contrary pull towards creating what we might call a 'composite' work. Put another way, he wanted to include both vaudeville and ballet in his scope, and accepted that this could not be achieved except at the cost of a loose story framework within which a wide range of different dance numbers were the real, yet diverse, core of the film. Every effort should be made to relate the embedded dance sequences to the dramatic story, but fundamentally his films were about dance, not about drama. Donen, although he came from a dance background, became increasingly involved in the non-dance aspects of film-making and, from the start, as he moved towards straight narrative films, he began to insist more on dramatic integration in the musical. In fact Donen came to dance through cinema, rather than the other way round like Kelly. As a child he was given an 8mm camera and a hand-cranked projector and his infatuation with dance stemmed from seeing Astaire in *Flying Down to Rio*. 'I sat there day in and day out watching that movie. I must have seen the picture thirty or forty times ... This led me to study dancing in my hometown as well as in New York.'[38] Donen was also a great admirer of Disney, with his pioneering synchronisation of music and movement in the 'Silly Symphonies'.

The relationship between film and dance was close from very early on. D. W. Griffith went to see Gertrude Hoffman's 'Saison des Ballets Russes' in 1911, featuring two 'Oriental' ballets, *Scheherazade* and *Cléopatra*, as well as the classical *Les Sylphides*. The next year Griffith hired Gertrude Bambrick away from Hoffman's Ballets Russes company to become his own resident dance expert. Her first job was to teach Griffith ragtime dancing, but she was also put to work on *The Mothering Heart* and *Judith of Bethulia*, which featured Assyrian dancing, choreographed by Bambrick, on the model of the 'Oriental' dancing earlier introduced by Hoffman herself (*Salomé*), Ruth St Denis (*Radha*) and the Ballets Russes (*Scheherazade*). Later, when Ruth St Denis and Ted Shawn opened their Denishawn dance school in Los Angeles, a close association was forged with Griffith, who attended the school himself and sent his actresses along as well – Blanche Sweet, who had been a professional dancer, and the Gish sisters, among others. The next year Griffith produced *Intolerance*, complete with vast dance sequences choreographed by Denishawn and led by Bambrick. DeMille and Ince also used Denishawn for similar orgiastic dancing sequences. Louise Glaum, Mae Murray, Mabel Normand and Florence Vidor all went to Denishawn, and others, like Carol Dempster, came from Denishawn to become stars. In the early silent period, there was an explicit affinity between pantomime acting and dance, which was not only demonstrated in spectacular dance sequences, but also inflected a whole style of acting. Among the great male stars, Rudolph Valentino had been a professional tango dancer before he came to Hollywood. 'A good dancer frequently makes a good screen actor,' said Michael Powell's model and mentor, the Irish director Rex Ingram.[39] It could even be argued that a dancer like Martha Graham, who emerged from Denishawn in Los Angeles and first became prominent in 1920 as the lead in *Xochitl*, a Ted Shawn vaudeville spectacle designed by the architect of the Maya Cinema, carried the aesthetic of early silent film into modern dance after it had been obliterated in Hollywood by the coming of sound.

In 1766, one hundred and fifty years before *Intolerance*, G. E.

Lessing wrote his path-breaking essay *Laocoon*, whose implications still resound through the history of twentieth-century art. Lessing argued that each of the arts had its own essential nature. Thus poetry used arbitrary signs successively, whereas painting used natural signs simultaneously. On this basis, he attacked the neo-classical doctrine of *ut pictura poesis*, the idea that painting and poetry shared the same goals and could be translated one into the other, so that poets could depict nature with words and painters could tell stories with images. Only poets, Lessing argued, could tell stories with extension in time and only painters could depict nature with a full sense of space. Lessing observed of the theatre, which combined words with spectacle, that 'the art of the actor occupies a middle position between the plastic arts and poetry', but he had nothing to say about dance, unlike his friend Moses Mendelssohn, who categorised dance as the only visual art in which signs (natural in dramatic dance, arbitrary in 'ordinary' dance) succeeded each other in time. (Cinema, of course, became the second visual art which could be defined in this way.) According to Mendelssohn, dance depended for its effect on 'the expression of beauty through movement', which Lessing characterised as 'charm'. Painting, for Lessing, could only suggest charm, since it could only suggest movement through the choice of a 'pregnant moment' in any ongoing action.[40]

In 1938 Rudolph Arnheim, a German writer on aesthetics then in exile, published his 'A New Laocoon: Artistic Composites and the Talking Film', looking at the cinema afresh in the light of Lessing's ideas. Arnheim argued that talking pictures had, for the most part, failed to solve the problem of their composite nature. Aesthetically, they derived from the merger of two previously independent forms – radio drama and silent film – each of which potentially had its own specific quality, as spoken language or imagery in motion, but which posed problems when an attempt was made to combine them. In particular, Arnheim lamented the dominance of dialogue on the soundtrack and the consequent loss of the specific aesthetic values of silent film. Like Lessing, Arnheim argued that each medium had its own specific characteristics, but, going further, that in the case of composite forms one medium must necessarily be dominant. In the theatre, verbal language is dominant and therefore, Arnheim argued, if film was to be distinct from drama, rather than just a form of recorded and expanded theatre, it should play to its own strongest suit and reverse the hierarchy, making the visual element dominant. As things stood, he claimed that 'dialogue paralyses visual action'. Film need not go back to silence, but it should reduce the role played by dialogue and move further towards being a predominantly visual art.

The root of the problem, as Arnheim saw it, was in the role played in the cinema by bodily acting (the visual dimension of acting). Silent film had relied on pantomime – 'dumb show', as it is called derisively by Kathy Selden in *Singin' in the Rain*. Arnheim argued that

> there is a limit to the visual expression that can be drawn from the human figure, particularly if the picture has to accompany dialogue. Pure pantomime knows of three ways to overcome this limitation. It can give up the portraying of plots and instead present the 'absolute' movement of the body, that is, dance. Here the human body becomes an instrument for melodic and harmonious forms, which are superior to mere pantomime, as music is superior to a (hypothetical) art of natural noises. Secondly, pantomime can adopt the solution of the silent film, namely become a part of the richer universe in motion [in which the human figure is placed on a level with that of non-speaking objects]. And, finally, it can become subservient to dramatic speech – as it does in the theatre. But to the pantomime of the talking film all three of these solutions are inaccessible: it cannot become dance, because dance does not need speech and perhaps does not even tolerate it; it cannot submerge in the huge *orbis pictus* of the silent film, because of its tie to the human figure; and it cannot become the servant of speech without giving up its own self.[41]

We can now see how a dance sequence like 'Singin' in the Rain' proposes a solution to Arnheim's dilemma. In effect, Kelly combines the first two of Arnheim's alternatives. Pantomime is elevated into dance, without entirely dispensing with a role for speech, which, in the form of song, serves both as an antechamber between dialogue and pure dance, and as a way of 'stating the thesis', so that the dance emerges out of speech. At the same time, the dance makes use of objects in the street – the umbrella, the lamp-post, the figure in the shop-window, the kerb, the puddle. Thus dance, the 'absolute' movement of the human body, which is paramount in the sequence, is linked through contextualisation and characterisation to the plot and, at the same time, the human body is integrated, through its gestures and movements, to the wider *orbis pictus* of inanimate objects.

The sequence is predominantly visual – the spectacle of the human body in motion – but it also makes use of speech and music. The movement is not completely 'arbitrary', as in 'pure' dance, but 'natural' or mimetic, staying in character, as far as possible. At the same time, the human body forms a kind of alliance with inanimate nature, making simple objects or features of the set into expressive, even at times anthropomorphic, props. Finally, the choreography of the human body is matched to the choreography of the camera, so that movement of the frame and movement within the frame are precisely articulated each with the other. This is precisely the kind of visually rich cinema that Arnheim was calling for. The problem for Kelly, however, was that of sustaining this strategy for the whole film, as he next tried to do in *Invitation to the Dance*, an experiment which inevitably ended up with filmed (and expanded) dance instead of filmed (and expanded) theatre. A sequence like 'Singin' in the Rain' could only work within what Arnheim calls a 'hybrid' form, one which varies the medium it privileges from sequence to sequence. The primary aesthetic problem then becomes that of transitions, rather than heterogeneity as such. Heterogeneity is aesthetically necessary.

This conclusion relates to another aspect of *Singin' in the Rain*. In their book *The Popular Arts*, Stuart Hall and Paddy Whannel describe how the crucial feature of the shift from folk art to popular art is the change which takes place in the nature of the contact between audience and performer. In the popular arts, a wider gap is opened up, and we see the beginnings of the great divide between audience and star, which is one of the themes of *Singin' in the Rain*. Yet the great popular artists, stars like Dickens, Marie Lloyd or Chaplin, emerge from the audience and retain the sense of community with it which characterised the performer of folk art. The popular arts can survive the transition into the mass media, as Chaplin did, but at the same time another process begins to create a form of 'mass art', which under the pressure of the market turns individual styles into packages, formulas or stereotypes. Nevertheless, popular art, they argue (in 1964), still survives in the mass media, in genres 'such as the western, the thriller and the musical', but 'this popular quality of the cinema is now threatened from both ends.' On the one hand, the rise of art film is transforming cinema from a popular to a 'high' art, and on the other hand, popular art is constantly in peril of declining into an exploitative 'mass art'.

This problem of the transfer from what was effectively an urban vernacular form of dancing to vaudeville to Broadway to Hollywood was precisely that which confronted Gene Kelly. How could he retain the popular appeal of tap, which he knew from his days in the clubs, while elevating it to the status of high art and expanding the audience to justify the production costs of a Hollywood film? Kelly realised, at each stage, that to succeed further meant rethinking the role of dance in each new context. Fundamentally, however, dance remained the focus of his artistic goals. But in order to succeed, artistically, in vaudeville or on Broadway or at the Freed Unit, he had to master the forms appropriate for a new mode of presentation or a new medium. Thus when he finally arrived in Hollywood he knew that in order to perfect his dance, he had to understand film and take charge of the filming of his own performance, a logic which led in the end to directing the whole film. At the same time, he understood that, just as on Broadway after *Oklahoma!* the 'dance director' had given way to the 'choreographer', so in Hollywood the 'film director' had to give way, in effect, to the 'cine-choreographer'.

Kelly's career was built as a performer, but, given the specialised nature of dance, he was compelled to become first a choreographer and then a film-maker, simply in order to realise his ambitions as a dancer. In fact, by the time he reached the summit of his career, his dancing days were on the way out. He was thirty-nine when he made *Singin' in the Rain*. Indeed, he attributes his longevity as a dancer to his excitement at finding a new field to conquer, which prolonged his physical mobility and energy beyond what he had a right to expect. Kelly's achievement was thus a multiple and composite one, as a dancer, as a choreographer, and as a film *auteur*. The first reflected his popular roots, the second his artistic ambition, and the third his hunger for a mass appeal.

The result was that Kelly succeeded in recapturing for the cinema an aesthetic which had almost been lost since the silent days. Arnheim noted that

> The films of the early years were less realistic and therefore expressed the various dramatic types by motions of graphic simplicity. There was musical purity and beauty in the graceful leaps of Douglas Fairbanks and the heavy stamping of Paul Wegener's Golem. Unquestionably the greater 'lifelikeness' of the later style has robbed the film play of much of its melodic shape. There was, in those dance-like pantomimes, a dance-like quality, which was most filmic and should not remain lost for ever.[42]

This was the quality which Kelly recaptured, in the 'graceful leaps' and 'heavy stamping' of 'Singin' in the Rain', pushing it beyond dance-like pantomime into dance itself. And, at the same time, by pushing the art of dance onto the terrain of film, he also took the art of cinema with him to new heights.

NOTES
....

1 Clive Hirschhorn, *Gene Kelly* (London: W. H. Allen, 1974, repr. 1984) p. 186.

2 Hirschhorn, pp. 67–8.

3 Richard Kislan, *Hoofing on Broadway, a History of Show Dancing* (New York: Prentice-Hall, 1987), p. 67.

4 Fred Astaire, *Steps in Time* (New York: Harper, 1959), p. 227.

5 Hirschhorn, p. 166.

6 David Martin, *The Films of Busby Berkeley* (San Francisco: David Martin, 1965), p. 7.

7 Hirschhorn, p. 100.

8 Joseph Andrew Casper, *Stanley Donen* (Metuchen, N.J. and London: Scarecrow Press, 1983), pp. 8–9.

9 Bertrand Tavernier and Daniel Palas, 'Entretien avec Stanley Donen', *Cahiers du Cinéma*, May 1963.

10 Hirschhorn, p. 109.

11 Debbie Reynolds, with David Patrick Columbia, *My Life* (London: Sidgwick & Jackson, 1989), p. 88.

12 Hirschhorn, p. 185.

13 Hirschhorn, p. 183.

14 Gerald Bordman, *American Operetta* (New York and Oxford: Oxford University Press, 1981).

15 Marshall and Jean Stearns, *Jazz Dance, The Story of American Vernacular Dance* (New York and London: Macmillan, 1968), p. 281.

16 See the interview with Fayard Nicholas in Rusty E. Frank, *Tap!* (New York: Morrow, 1990).

17 Powell's interest in ballet as expressed in *The Red Shoes* combined an interest in the dance element of silent film with his commitment to a neo-romantic modernism and his childhood attachment to the Mediterranean coast resorts.

18 Betty Comden and Adolph Green, *Singin' in the Rain* (London: Lorrimer, 1986), p. 63.

19 Hirschhorn, p. 188.

20 Hirschhorn, p. 204.

21 Hirschhorn, p. 64.

22 Hirschhorn, p. 132.

23 Hirschhorn, p. 82.

24 Hirschhorn, p. 135.

25 Hirschhorn, p. 135.

26 Whitney Balliet, 'Profiles: Night Clubs', *New Yorker*, 9 October 1971.

27 Malcolm Goldstein, *The Political Stage* (New York: Oxford University Press, 1964), p. 205.

28 See references in bibliography.

29 John Cogley, *Report on Blacklisting, I. Movies* (The Fund for the Republic, n.p., 1956), p. 159.

30 Gary Carey, *Judy Holliday, An Intimate Life Story* (New York: Seaview Books, 1986), p. 33.

31 Rudy Behlmer, *America's Favorite Movies: Behind the Scenes* (London: Samuel French, 1990), p. 264.

32 Hugh Fordin, *The World of Entertainment* (Garden City: Doubleday, 1975), p. 355.

33 Rick Altman, *The American Film Musical* (Bloomington and London: Indiana University Press and BFI Publishing, 1989), p. 272.

34 Reynolds, p. 89.

35 Comden and Green, p. 45.

36 Casper, p. 34

37 Stuart Hall and Paddy Whannel, *The Popular Arts* (London: Hutchinson, 1964).

38 Casper, p. 4.

39 Elizabeth Kendall, *Where She Danced* (New York: Knopf, 1979), p. 142.

40 See David E. Wellbury, *Lessing's Laocoon* (Cambridge: Cambridge University Press, 1984).

41 Rudolph Arnheim, *Film as Art* (London: Faber & Faber, 1983), pp. 186–7.

42 Arnheim, p. 152.

CREDITS

Singin' in the Rain

USA
1951
Production company
Loew's Incorporated
US release
1952
Distributor
MGM
UK release
1952
Copyright date
1951
Producer
Arthur Freed
Directors
Gene Kelly, Stanley Donen
Screenplay
Betty Comden, Adolph
Green from their own story
Photography (Technicolor)
Harold Rosson
Musical direction
Lennie Hayton
Orchestral arrangements
Wally Heglin, Skip Martin,
Conrad Salinger
Vocal arrangements
Jeff Alexander
Roger Edens (uncredited)

Songs
'Would you?', 'Singin' in the
Rain', 'All I do is dream of
you', 'I've got a feeling
you're fooling', 'Wedding of
the painted doll', 'Should I?',
'Make 'em laugh', 'Beautiful
girl', 'You were meant for
me', 'You are my lucky
star', 'Good morning',
'Broadway rhythm',
'Broadway melody' by
Arthur Freed (lyrics), Nacio
Herb Brown (music); 'Fit as
a fiddle and ready for love'
by Al Hoffman, Al
Goodhart (music), Arthur
Freed (lyrics); 'Moses' by
Roger Edens (music), Betty
Comden, Adolph Green
(lyrics)
**Staging and direction of
musical numbers**
Gene Kelly, Stanley Donen
Editor
Adrienne Fazan
Art direction
Cedric Gibbons, Randall
Duell
Set decoration
Edwin B. Willis, Jacques
Mapes
Costume design
Walter Plunkett
Make-up
William Tuttle
Hairstyles
Sydney Guilaroff
**Special photographic
effects**
Warren Newcombe, Irving
G. Ries
Colour consultants
Henri Jaffa, James Gooch
Recording supervisor
Douglas Shearer

Associate producer
Roger Edens
Camera operator
Frank Phillips
**Assistants to the
choreographer**
Carol Haney, Jeanne Coyne
103 minutes
9,300 feet

Gene Kelly
Don Lockwood
Donald O'Connor
Cosmo Brown
Debbie Reynolds
Kathy Selden
Jean Hagen
Lina Lamont
Millard Mitchell
R. F. Simpson
Cyd Charisse
Dancer in ballet
Douglas Fowley
Roscoe Dexter
Rita Moreno
Zelda Zanders
Madge Blake
Dora Bailey
King Donovan
Rod
Kathleen Freeman
Phoebe Dinsmore, diction coach
Bobby Watson
Diction coach
Tommy Farrell
Sid Phillips, assistant director
Jimmie Thompson
*Male lead in 'Beautiful Girl'
number*

Dan Foster
Assistant director
Margaret Bert
Wardrobe woman
Mae Clarke
Hairdresser
Judy Landon
Olga Mara
John Dodsworth
Baron de la Bouvet de la Toulon
Stuart Holmes
J. C. Spendrill III
Dennis Ross
Don as a boy
Bill Lewin
Bert, villain in Western
Richard Emory
Phil, cowboy hero
Julius Tannen
Man in talking picture demonstration
Dawn Addams
Teresa, lady-in-waiting
Elaine Stewart
Second lady-in-waiting
Carl Milletaire
Villain in 'The Duelling Cavalier' and 'Broadway Rhythm'
Ben Strombach
Pilot in flying film
Tommy Walker
Footballer in film sequence
Jac George
Orchestra leader
Wilson Wood
Rudy Vallee impersonator
Brick Sullivan
Cop in title number

Snub Pollard
Recipient of umbrella at end of title number
Paul Maxey
Sceptical party guest
Dorothy Patrick
William Lester
Joi Lansing
Spectators
Charles Evans
Irritated spectator
Dave Sharpe
Russ Saunders
Fencers
Patricia Denise
Jeanne Coyne
Joyce Horne
Dancers
Bill Chatham
Ernest Flatt
Don Hulbert
Robert Dayo
David Kasday
Kid
Robert B. Williams
Traffic cop
Ray Teal
Employee

The print of *Singin' in the Rain* in the National Film Archive was specially acquired from Turner Entertainment.

(Credits prepared by Markku Salmi)

BIBLIOGRAPHY

The script of *Singin' in the Rain*, by Betty Comden and Adolph Green, is published by Lorrimer (London, 1986), with an introduction by the authors. The two principal sources on the film's production background are Hugh Fordin, *The World of Entertainment!* (Garden City: Doubleday, 1975), which is a thoroughly researched history of the Freed Unit at MGM, dealing specifically with *Singin' in the Rain*, pp. 347–62; and Rudy Behlmer, *America's Favorite Movies: Behind the Scenes* (London: Samuel French, 1990), which has a useful chapter on the making of *Singin' in the Rain*, pp. 253–68. John Mariani, 'Come on with the Rain', in *Film Comment*, May–June 1978, also contains interesting information.

Biographies provide invaluable material, especially Clive Hirschhorn, *Gene Kelly* (London: W. H. Allen, 1974, repr. 1984), which is serious and detailed, with a number of long and important quotes from interviews with Kelly himself. I also consulted Tony Thomas, *The Films of Gene Kelly* (New York: Citadel, 1991). Kelly inveighs against the *auteur* theory in his interview in Andrew Britton (ed.), *Talking Films* (London: Fourth Estate, 1991). Joseph Andrew Casper, *Stanley*

Donen (Metuchen, N.J., and London: Scarecrow Press, 1983) contains a thoughtful account of Donen's career, making a case for him as an *auteur*, with many quotes from Donen himself. I also quote from an excellent interview with Donen by Bertrand Tavernier and Daniel Palas, published in *Cahiers du Cinéma*, May 1963.

Comden and Green are interviewed in Pat McGilligan, *Backstory 2* (Berkeley: University of California, 1991). For their early career with The Revuers, see Max Gordon, *Live At The Village Vanguard* (New York: St. Martin's Press, 1980) and Gary Carey, *Judy Holliday, An Intimate Life Story* (New York: Seaview Books, 1986), and, for their place in Popular Front culture and the quote from *TAC* magazine, Malcolm Goldstein, *The Political Stage* (New York: Oxford University Press, 1964). I also quote Max Gordon talking to Whitney Balliett, in 'Profiles: Night Clubs', published in the *New Yorker*, 9 October 1971.

For Debbie Reynolds, see Debbie Reynolds, with David Patrick Columbia, *My Life* (London: Sidgwick & Jackson, 1989) and for Cyd Charisse, her joint life-story, Tony Martin and Cyd Charisse, as told to Dick Kleiner, *The Two of Us* (New York: Mason Charter, 1976). The best source for Donald O'Connor is the interview in Rusty E. Frank, *Tap!* (New York: Morrow, 1990), which also contains an interview with Gene Kelly's brother, Fred, as well as Ann Miller, Fayard Nicholas and several other Hollywood dancers.

The World of Entertainment! gives some frustratingly sparse information on the early careers of Arthur Freed and Nacio Herb Brown, for which also see David A. Jasen, *Tin Pan Alley* (New York: Donald I. Fine, 1988). There is still no comprehensive history of American popular music. For the coming of sound in Hollywood, see Elisabeth Weis and John Belton (eds.), *Film Sound: Theory and Practice* (New York: Columbia University Press, 1985), which has a full bibliography.

The best history of tap dancing is still Marshall and Jean Stearns, *Jazz Dance, The Story of American Vernacular Dance* (New York and London: Macmillan, 1968). This is primarily a history of black dancing and, for the white dancers in their debt, needs to be supplemented by *Tap!* and by Richard Kislan, *Hoofing on Broadway, A History of Show Dancing* (New York: Prentice-Hall, 1987), which I drew on especially for material on John Alton. Readers who feel like trying out a few tap steps might consult Tina Marx, *Tap Dance, A Beginner's Guide* (Englewood Cliffs, N.J.: Prentice-Hall, 1983).

For ballet in America, see Lynn Garafola, *Diaghilev's Ballets Russes* (New York and Oxford: Oxford University Press, 1989) and Olga Maynard, *The American Ballet* (Philadelphia: Macrae Smith, 1959). Edwin Denby, *Dance Writings* (New York: Knopf, 1986) collects together dance reviews which Denby wrote during the period that Kelly was in New York. The early story of modern dance in America, especially in relation to Hollywood, is told with erudition and verve in Elizabeth Kendall, *Where She Danced* (New York: Knopf, 1979), and Margaret Lloyd, *The Borzoi Book of Modern Dance* (New

York: Knopf, 1949) carries the story on as far as Kelly's early films.

Gerald Mast, *Can't Help Singin'* (Woodstock: Overlook Press, 1987), provides a detailed historical introduction to the musical, encompassing both stage and screen. Rick Altman (ed.), *Genre: The Musical* (London: Routledge & Kegan Paul/BFI, 1981), brings together some of the best essays on the film musical as a genre, and Jane Feuer, *The Hollywood Musical* (London: BFI/Macmillan, 1982), is a provocative introduction to the genre, combining theoretical insight with passionate love of the films. Rick Altman, *The American Film Musical* (Bloomington and London: Indiana University Press and BFI Publishing, 1989), is a model of genre study: comprehensive, illuminating and scholarly. For Busby Berkeley, see David Martin, *The Films of Busby Berkeley* (San Francisco: David Martin, 1965), and for Astaire and radio, Fred Astaire, *Steps in Time* (New York: Harper, 1959). Parker Tyler, *Magic and Myth of the Movies* (New York: Henry Holt, 1947), vividly evokes the surrealist dimension of Hollywood.

The stage musical has been less well served. See, however, three books by Gerald Bordman: *American Operetta* (New York and Oxford: Oxford University Press, 1981), *American Musical Comedy* (New York and Oxford: Oxford University Press, 1982) and *American Musical Revue* (New York and Oxford: Oxford University Press, 1985). I also drew on Cecil Smith, *Musical Comedy in America* (New York: Theatre Arts Books, 1950), and Ethan Mordden, *Better Foot Forward* (New York: Viking, 1976). John Martin's comments on *Pal Joey* are cited in *Hoofing on Broadway*.

For the purge of the left in Hollywood, I have consulted, for Alvin Hammer, his testimony on 16 May 1951, to the US Congress House Committee on UnAmerican Activities, *Communist Infiltration of Hollywood Motion-Picture Industry – Part 1* (Washington: US Government Printing Office, 1951); for Adolph Green, Harvey Matusow's testimony on 6 February 1952, to the same Committee, *Communist Activity among Youth Groups* (Washington, 1952), looking also at Harvey Matusow, *False Witness* (New York: Cameron & Kahn, 1952); and, for Judy Holliday, her testimony on 28 March 1952, to the

Senate Subcommittee to Investigate the Administration of the Internal Security Act and other Internal Security Laws, of the Committee on the Judiciary, *Subversive Infiltration of Radio, Television, and the Entertainment Industry* (Washington, 1952), as well as Gary Carey's informative biography.

Edward L. Barrett, Jr., *The Tenney Committee* (Ithaca, N.Y.: Cornell University Press, 1951), describes the work of the Committee and includes Kelly's letter of rebuttal to the Committee's findings on him, addressed to the author and dated 30 July 1949. David Caute, *The Great Fear* (New York: Simon & Schuster, 1978), notes how Jack Tenney made Kelly 'one of his frequent targets' (p. 490) and also how Roy Brewer 'negotiated the repentance, confession and final clearance' of Kelly (p. 502). For the *American Legion Magazine*'s listing of *Singin' in the Rain*, see Caute (pp. 503 and 615). John Cogley, *Report on Blacklisting, I. Movies* (The Fund for the Republic: n.p., 1956), notes that Kelly 'had been so harassed that he went off to Europe' and cites his apology and commendation of Brewer before the AFL Council (p. 159). Larry Ceplair and Steven Englund, *The Inquisition in Hollywood* (Berkeley and Los Angeles:

University of California Press, 1983), is still the best comprehensive account of the period, with a number of references to Kelly. For Kelly and Holliday specifically, see also the Hirschhorn and Carey biographies, although Hirschhorn, in my view, does not reveal the whole story and should be read in the context of the other studies cited.

In the field of aesthetics and semiotics, for Gotthold Ephraim Lessing see his *Laocoon* (London: Dent, 1930), and David E. Wellbury, *Lessing's Laocoon* (Cambridge: Cambridge University Press, 1984), which also has a valuable section on Mendelssohn. Rudolph Arnheim's 'A New Laocoon' is reprinted in his *Film as Art* (London: Faber & Faber, 1983). For Victor Shklovsky, see his *Theory of Prose* (Elmwood Park, Ill.: Dalkey Archive Press, 1990). Finally, I come to Stuart Hall and Paddy Whannel, *The Popular Arts* (London: Hutchinson, 1964). I first read this path-breaking book back in 1964, when it was originally published in Britain. Together with many subsequent discussions of Hollywood movies and many viewings of *Singin' in the Rain* with Paddy Whannel, it decisively shaped my own thought on the cinema.

BFI Publishing
21 Stephen Street
FREEPOST 7
LONDON
W1E 4AN